HOW TO START A LAUNDROMAT BUSINESS

Your Ultimate Guide to Launching, Managing, and Growing a Successful Laundry Shop (Even with Small or Zero Capital)

James Roland

All rights reserved. No part of this publication may be reproduced in any form or by any means, including photocopying, recording, or any other electronic or mechanical methods without the prior written permission of the publisher except in the case of brief quotations embodied in reviews and certain other non-commercial uses permitted by copyrights law.

Copyright © James Roland, 2024.

Table of Contents

INTRODUCTION   7

Chapter 1   9

The Laundromat Landscape – Your First Spin Cycle into Laundry Entrepreneurship   9
- 1.1 Why Laundromats Are a Smart Business Investment   10
- 1.2 The Current State of the Laundromat Industry   11
- 1.3 Types of Laundromat Models   12
- 1.4 Assessing Your Local Market and Competition   13
- 1.5 Identifying Your Target Customer Base   15
- 1.6 The Financial Potential of a Laundromat Business   16
- 1.7 Setting Realistic Expectations for Success   17

Chapter 2   19

Creating Your Laundromat Business Plan – Laying the Foundation for Laundry Success   19
- 2.1 Defining Your Laundromat Vision and Mission   20
- 2.2 Choosing a Business Structure   21
- 2.3 Outlining Startup Costs and Financial Projections   23
- 2.4 Developing a Marketing and Branding Strategy   24
- 2.5 Creating a Pricing Structure for Your Services   26
- 2.6 Writing a Comprehensive Business Plan   27
- 2.7 Securing Funding and Investment (Even with Limited Capital)   28

Chapter 3   31

Finding the Perfect Location – Where Laundry Dreams Take Root   31
- 3.1 Evaluating Ideal Laundromat Locations   32
- 3.2 Analyzing Demographics and Foot Traffic   33
- 3.3 Negotiating Lease Terms and Agreements   35
- 3.4 Obtaining Necessary Permits and Licenses   36
- 3.5 Understanding Zoning Regulations   37
- 3.6 Designing Your Laundromat Layout for Efficiency   38

3.7 Ensuring Accessibility and Safety for Customers   41

Chapter 4   43

Equipping Your Laundromat – Building the Heart of Your Laundry Haven   43

    4.1 Choosing the Right Washers and Dryers   44
    4.2 Selecting Additional Equipment   46
    4.3 Budgeting for Maintenance and Repairs   47
    4.4 Finding Reliable Suppliers and Vendors   49
    4.5 Installing Energy-Efficient Systems   50
    4.6 Implementing Security Measures   52
    4.7 Creating a Comfortable and Inviting Atmosphere   53

Chapter 5   56

Launching Your Laundromat – The Grand Unveiling of Your Laundry Haven   56

    5.1 Developing a Grand Opening Marketing Plan   57
    5.2 Creating a Memorable Launch Event   58
    5.3 Implementing Effective Pricing Strategies   60
    5.4 Building Customer Loyalty Programs   62
    5.5 Utilizing Social Media and Online Marketing   64
    5.6 Partnering with Local Businesses   66
    5.7 Tracking Key Performance Indicators (KPIs)   67

Chapter 6   70

Day-to-Day Laundromat Operations – The Rhythm of Laundry Life   70

    6.1 Hiring and Training Staff (If Applicable)   70
    6.2 Managing Inventory and Supplies   73
    6.3 Implementing Efficient Cleaning Procedures   74
    6.4 Handling Customer Complaints and Issues   76
    6.5 Ensuring a Safe and Secure Environment   77
    6.6 Utilizing Technology to Streamline Operations   80
    6.7 Staying Up-to-Date on Industry Trends   81

Chapter 7   83

Marketing and Growing Your Laundromat – Spinning Your Way to Success   83
    7.1 Building a Strong Brand Identity   84
    7.2 Creating Effective Marketing Campaigns   86
    7.3 Utilizing Online and Offline Advertising   88
    7.4 Leveraging Social Media for Engagement   91
    7.5 Offering Special Promotions and Discounts   93
    7.6 Expanding Your Services   94
    7.7 Building Strategic Partnerships   96

Chapter 8   98

Managing Finances and Maximizing Profit – The Art of Laundry Economics   98
    8.1 Understanding Laundromat Financial Statements   98
    8.2 Tracking Revenue and Expenses   100
    8.3 Implementing Pricing Strategies   101
    8.4 Budgeting for Growth and Expansion   103
    8.5 Managing Cash Flow Effectively   104
    8.6 Utilizing Accounting Software   105
    8.7 Minimizing Taxes and Legal Liabilities   107

Chapter 9   110

Ensuring Legal Compliance – Navigating the Legal Landscape of Laundromat Ownership   110
    9.1 Obtaining Necessary Business Licenses and Permits 111
    9.2 Complying with Local and Federal Regulations   113
    9.3 Protecting Your Intellectual Property   114
    9.4 Understanding Insurance Requirements   116
    9.5 Handling Employee Matters (If Applicable)   117
    9.6 Navigating Tax Obligations   119
    9.7 Staying Informed on Legal Changes   121

Chapter 10   123

Technology and Innovation in Laundromats – The Digital Transformation of Laundry Day   123

- 10.1 Leveraging Laundromat Management Software   124
- 10.2 Implementing Mobile Payment Options   126
- 10.3 Utilizing Online Booking Systems   128
- 10.4 Exploring Smart Laundry Solutions   130
- 10.5 Enhancing Customer Experience with Technology 132
- 10.6 Staying Ahead of the Curve with Innovation   134
- 10.7 Embracing Eco-Friendly Practices   136

Chapter 11   139

Overcoming Challenges and Troubleshooting – Weathering the Storms of Laundromat Ownership   139

- 11.1 Dealing with Equipment Malfunctions   140
- 11.2 Handling Difficult Customers   141
- 11.3 Managing Competition   143
- 11.4 Adapting to Economic Fluctuations   145
- 11.5 Addressing Security Concerns   147
- 11.6 Maintaining High Hygiene Standards   149
- 11.7 Resolving Operational Issues   151

Chapter 12   153

Scaling and Expanding Your Laundromat Empire – From Single Spin Cycle to Laundry Dynasty   153

- 12.1 Evaluating Growth Opportunities   154
- 12.2 Opening Additional Locations   155
- 12.3 Franchising Your Laundromat Business   157
- 12.4 Exploring New Revenue Streams   159

INTRODUCTION

Have you ever dreamed of owning your own business, one that's recession-proof and offers a steady income stream? If so, a laundromat might be the perfect fit for you.

Laundromats are a classic example of a business that provides an essential service – clean clothes – that people will always need. They thrive in both booming economies and tough times, making them a resilient and potentially lucrative venture.

But starting a laundromat can seem daunting. Where do you begin? How do you find the right location, secure funding, choose the right equipment, and attract a loyal customer base?

That's where this book comes in. **"How to Start a Laundromat Business: Your Ultimate Guide to Launching, Managing, and Growing a Successful Laundry Shop (Even with Small or Zero Capital)"** is your comprehensive roadmap to laundromat success.

Whether you're a seasoned entrepreneur or a first-time business owner, this guide will walk you through every step of the process, from initial concept to grand opening and beyond. We'll cover everything you need to know, including:

- **Market research:** How to assess your local market and identify your target audience

- **Business planning:** Crafting a solid business plan that outlines your goals, strategies, and financial projections
- **Funding options:** Securing financing, even with limited capital
- **Location selection:** Finding the perfect spot for your laundromat
- **Equipment selection:** Choosing the right washers, dryers, and other essential equipment
- **Marketing and promotion:** Attracting and retaining customers
- **Day-to-day operations:** Managing staff, inventory, and finances
- **Growth strategies:** Expanding your services and scaling your business

Even if you're starting with a small budget or no capital at all, this book will show you how to overcome financial obstacles and build a thriving laundromat. We'll share insider tips, real-world examples, and practical advice that will help you avoid common pitfalls and achieve your entrepreneurial dreams.

So, if you're ready to turn your laundromat vision into reality, let's dive in! This book is your key to unlocking the secrets of laundromat success.

Chapter 1

The Laundromat Landscape – Your First Spin Cycle into Laundry Entrepreneurship

Imagine this: a bustling street corner, the comforting hum of machines, the scent of freshly laundered clothes wafting through the air. This is the heart of a laundromat, a place where everyday life intersects with a simple yet essential service. But beyond the spinning drums and folding tables lies a world of opportunity, a chance to build a thriving business that caters to a universal need.

Welcome to the first chapter of our laundromat adventure, where we'll immerse ourselves in the vibrant landscape of this industry. We'll uncover the reasons why laundromats are a smart business investment, delve into the current state of the industry, and explore the diverse models that have emerged over time. We'll also learn how to assess your local market, identify your ideal customers, and understand the financial potential that awaits you. By the end of this chapter, you'll have a solid foundation for your journey into laundromat entrepreneurship.

1.1 Why Laundromats Are a Smart Business Investment

In a world of ever-changing trends and fleeting fads, laundromats stand as a testament to stability and resilience. They provide a fundamental service that transcends economic fluctuations and demographic shifts. Clean clothes are a necessity, not a luxury, and as long as people wear clothes, there will be a demand for laundromats.

Here's a closer look at why laundromats are a smart business investment:

- **Recession-Proof:** Unlike many industries that suffer during economic downturns, laundromats often experience steady or even increased demand. When budgets tighten, people may forgo dry cleaning but still need to wash their everyday clothes.
- **Consistent Revenue Stream:** Laundromats generate revenue through a variety of channels, including self-service machines, wash-and-fold services, and vending machines. This diversification helps to ensure a consistent income flow.
- **Low Employee Turnover:** Compared to other service-based businesses, laundromats typically have lower employee turnover. Many laundromats are self-service, requiring minimal staffing.
- **Flexible Business Model:** Laundromats can be adapted to various business models, from

small, coin-operated facilities to larger, full-service establishments. This flexibility allows you to tailor your business to your specific market and resources.
- **Scalability:** If you start with a single location and find success, you can expand your laundromat empire by opening additional branches or offering new services.

1.2 The Current State of the Laundromat Industry

The laundromat industry has evolved significantly over the years, adapting to changing consumer preferences and technological advancements. While traditional coin-operated laundromats still exist, many modern establishments offer a range of amenities and services to enhance the customer experience.

Here's the current state of the laundromat industry:

- **Technological Integration:** Many laundromats have embraced technology, offering mobile payment options, online booking systems, and smart laundry solutions that allow customers to monitor their laundry cycles remotely.
- **Increased Focus on Customer Experience:** Laundromat owners are recognizing the importance of providing a clean, comfortable, and convenient environment for their customers. This includes amenities like free Wi-Fi, seating areas, and even coffee shops.

- **Rise of Wash-and-Fold Services:** The convenience of wash-and-fold services, where customers drop off their laundry to be washed, dried, and folded by staff, has become increasingly popular, particularly among busy professionals and families.
- **Sustainability Initiatives:** Many laundromats are adopting eco-friendly practices, such as using energy-efficient machines, offering reusable laundry bags, and implementing water conservation measures.
- **Diverse Ownership:** The laundromat industry is increasingly diverse, with entrepreneurs from various backgrounds entering the market. This diversity brings fresh perspectives and innovative ideas to the industry.

1.3 Types of Laundromat Models

Laundromats come in various shapes and sizes, each with its own unique characteristics and target audience. Here are the three main types of laundromat models:

1. **Self-Serve Laundromats:** The classic coin-operated laundromat is still a popular option. These facilities provide customers with washers, dryers, and basic amenities like folding tables and detergent vending machines. Self-serve laundromats require minimal staffing and are often open 24/7, making them convenient for customers with busy schedules.

2. **Wash-and-Fold Laundromats:** This model offers customers the convenience of dropping off their laundry to be washed, dried, and folded by staff. Wash-and-fold services are particularly popular among busy professionals, families, and individuals who prefer not to spend time doing laundry themselves. These laundromats may also offer pickup and delivery services for added convenience.
3. **Full-Service Laundromats:** These establishments provide a comprehensive range of laundry services, including self-service machines, wash-and-fold, dry cleaning, and even alterations. Full-service laundromats cater to a wider customer base and often offer additional amenities like Wi-Fi, coffee shops, and children's play areas.

The type of laundromat you choose will depend on your budget, target market, and personal preferences. Each model has its own advantages and disadvantages, and it's essential to weigh your options carefully before making a decision.

1.4 Assessing Your Local Market and Competition

Before diving headfirst into the laundromat business, it's crucial to assess your local market and understand your competition. This will help you identify opportunities, anticipate challenges, and develop a winning strategy.

Here's how to assess your local market and competition:

- **Demographic Analysis:** Start by researching the demographics of your target area. Consider factors like population density, income levels, age distribution, and household size. This information will help you determine the demand for laundromat services and tailor your offerings accordingly.
- **Competitive Landscape:** Identify existing laundromats in your area and analyze their strengths and weaknesses. Visit their facilities, observe their operations, and assess their pricing, services, and amenities. This will give you valuable insights into what works and what doesn't in your local market.
- **Identifying Gaps in the Market:** Look for unmet needs or underserved segments in your community. Are there areas with a high concentration of apartment buildings or college students who lack access to convenient laundry facilities? Are there opportunities to offer specialized services like pet-friendly washing or commercial laundry?

By thoroughly analyzing your local market and competition, you can position your laundromat for success and differentiate yourself from the crowd.

1.5 Identifying Your Target Customer Base

Understanding your target customer base is essential for tailoring your services, marketing efforts, and overall business strategy. Different demographics have varying laundry needs and preferences, and it's crucial to cater to their specific requirements.

Here are some key factors to consider when identifying your target customer base:

- **Demographics:** Consider the age, income level, occupation, and household size of your potential customers. For example, young professionals and students may prioritize convenience and affordability, while families may value larger machines and kid-friendly amenities.
- **Lifestyle:** Think about the lifestyle of your target customers. Are they busy professionals who value time-saving solutions like wash-and-fold services? Are they environmentally conscious individuals who prefer eco-friendly laundromats?
- **Location:** The location of your laundromat will also influence your target customer base. If you're located near a college campus, you'll likely attract students, while a laundromat in a residential area may cater to families and retirees.

Once you've identified your target customer base, you can tailor your services, pricing, and marketing efforts to meet their needs and preferences, ultimately driving customer loyalty and satisfaction.

1.6 The Financial Potential of a Laundromat Business

The financial potential of a laundromat business can vary depending on various factors, including location, size, services offered, and operational efficiency. However, with careful planning and effective management, laundromats can generate a healthy profit margin.

Here's a glimpse into the financial potential of a laundromat business:

- **Revenue Streams:** Laundromats generate revenue through multiple channels, including self-service machine usage, wash-and-fold services, vending machines, and additional offerings like dry cleaning or alterations.
- **Profit Margins:** The profit margin for laundromats typically ranges from 20% to 35%, depending on various factors. However, some well-managed laundromats can achieve even higher profit margins.
- **Return on Investment (ROI):** The average ROI for a laundromat is estimated to be between 10% and 25%. However, this can vary significantly depending on the initial investment, operating costs, and revenue generation.

It's important to note that the financial success of a laundromat is not guaranteed. It requires careful planning, effective management, and a commitment to providing excellent customer service. However, with the right approach, a laundromat can be a lucrative and rewarding business venture.

1.7 Setting Realistic Expectations for Success

While the laundromat industry offers promising opportunities, it's crucial to set realistic expectations for success. Building a thriving laundromat takes time, effort, and dedication. It's not a get-rich-quick scheme but rather a long-term investment that requires careful planning and consistent management. It's about understanding your market, adapting to change, and providing a service that truly benefits your community.

As you embark on this exciting journey, remember that success in the laundromat business isn't solely measured by financial gain. It's also about the satisfaction of building a business that provides a valuable service to your community, creating jobs, and fostering a sense of connection among your customers.

In the following chapters, we'll delve deeper into the intricacies of starting and running a laundromat business. We'll explore topics like creating a comprehensive business plan, securing funding, finding the perfect location, selecting the right equipment, and marketing your laundromat effectively. We'll also discuss the day-to-day operations, financial management, legal compliance, and strategies for scaling and expanding your business.

But for now, take a moment to envision your ideal laundromat. Picture the bright, clean space, the satisfied customers folding their laundry, and the sense of pride you'll feel as the owner of a thriving business. This vision will serve as your guiding light as you navigate the exciting and sometimes challenging path of laundromat entrepreneurship.

Remember, this is just the beginning of your journey. With the right knowledge, resources, and determination, you can turn your laundromat dream into a reality. So, let's roll up our sleeves and dive deeper into the world of laundry!

Chapter 2

Creating Your Laundromat Business Plan – Laying the Foundation for Laundry Success

Welcome to the second spin cycle of your laundromat journey! In this chapter, we'll delve into the crucial process of creating a comprehensive business plan for your laundromat. Think of it as your roadmap to success, a detailed blueprint that outlines your vision, strategies, and financial projections.

A well-crafted business plan is essential for several reasons. First, it helps you clarify your goals and objectives, ensuring that everyone involved in the venture is on the same page. Second, it serves as a valuable tool for securing funding from investors or lenders. Third, it acts as a guide for making informed decisions and navigating the inevitable challenges that arise during the startup and growth phases of your business.

In this chapter, we'll cover everything you need to know to create a winning laundromat business plan, including defining your vision and mission, choosing a business structure, outlining startup costs and financial projections, developing a marketing and branding strategy, creating a pricing structure, and securing funding, even with limited capital.

So, grab a pen and paper (or your favorite digital note-taking app) and let's get started on building the foundation for your laundromat empire.

2.1 Defining Your Laundromat Vision and Mission

Before you dive into the nitty-gritty details of your business plan, it's important to take a step back and define your vision and mission for your laundromat. Your vision is your long-term aspiration, the ultimate goal you want to achieve with your business. Your mission, on the other hand, is your purpose, the reason why you're starting this venture.

Here are some questions to consider when defining your vision and mission:

- **What impact do you want to make in your community?** Do you want to provide a convenient and affordable laundry solution for your neighbors? Are you passionate about creating a welcoming space where people can connect and build community?
- **What values are important to you and your business?** Do you prioritize sustainability, customer service, or innovation?
- **What sets your laundromat apart from the competition?** Are you offering unique services, a specific atmosphere, or a focus on a particular niche market?

Your vision and mission should be concise, compelling, and reflect your passion for the laundromat business. They will serve as guiding principles throughout your entrepreneurial journey, helping you make decisions that align with your core values and goals.

For example, your vision statement might be: "To create the most welcoming and technologically advanced laundromat in the city, providing a superior customer experience and fostering a sense of community."

Your mission statement could be: "To offer convenient, affordable, and eco-friendly laundry solutions to our community while creating a warm and inviting space for people to connect."

Once you've defined your vision and mission, you can move on to the next step of your business plan: choosing a business structure.

2.2 Choosing a Business Structure

The business structure you choose for your laundromat will have legal and financial implications, so it's important to understand your options and select the one that best suits your needs.

Here are the most common business structures for laundromats:

1. **Sole Proprietorship:** This is the simplest and most common business structure. As a sole proprietor, you are personally liable for all debts and obligations of the business. However,

you have complete control over the business and all profits belong to you.
2. **Partnership:** A partnership involves two or more individuals sharing ownership and responsibility for the business. Partnerships can be general (where all partners share equal liability) or limited (where some partners have limited liability).
3. **Limited Liability Company (LLC):** An LLC offers the limited liability protection of a corporation with the tax benefits of a partnership. This structure is popular among small business owners because it offers flexibility and protection from personal liability.
4. **Corporation:** A corporation is a separate legal entity from its owners, which means that shareholders are not personally liable for the company's debts. Corporations are more complex to set up and maintain than other business structures, but they offer the advantage of raising capital through the sale of stock.

The best business structure for your laundromat will depend on your personal circumstances, risk tolerance, and long-term goals. It's advisable to consult with an attorney or accountant to determine the most suitable option for your specific situation.

2.3 Outlining Startup Costs and Financial Projections

One of the most critical components of your laundromat business plan is outlining your startup costs and financial projections. This will give you a clear picture of the financial investment required to launch your business and help you secure funding from investors or lenders.

Here's a breakdown of typical startup costs for a laundromat:

- **Lease or purchase of a location:** This is usually the most significant expense. The cost will vary depending on the size and location of the property.
- **Equipment:** This includes washers, dryers, vending machines, change machines, folding tables, and other necessary equipment. Consider both new and used options to manage costs.
- **Permits and licenses:** You'll need to obtain various permits and licenses to operate a laundromat, which can vary depending on your location.
- **Utilities:** Laundromats consume a significant amount of water and electricity, so factor in these costs.
- **Insurance:** Business insurance is essential to protect your investment and mitigate risks.
- **Marketing and advertising:** Allocate a budget for marketing your laundromat and attracting customers.
- **Initial inventory:** This includes detergent, fabric softener, laundry bags, and other supplies.
- **Operating expenses:** Factor in ongoing expenses like rent, utilities, payroll, maintenance, and repairs.

Once you've estimated your startup costs, it's time to create financial projections. This involves forecasting your revenue and expenses over a specific period, usually three to five years. Your projections should be based on realistic assumptions and should include a break-even analysis, which shows when your business is expected to become profitable.

Accurate financial projections are crucial for securing funding and demonstrating the viability of your business to potential investors or lenders. Be sure to research industry averages and consult with financial professionals to ensure your projections are realistic and well-supported.

2.4 Developing a Marketing and Branding Strategy

In the competitive laundromat landscape, a strong marketing and branding strategy is essential for attracting and retaining customers. Your brand is more than just a logo or a slogan; it's the overall perception that customers have of your business.

Here are some key elements of a successful laundromat marketing and branding strategy:

- **Brand Identity:** Develop a unique brand identity that reflects your values, target audience, and the overall experience you want to create for your customers. This includes your logo, color scheme, messaging, and overall aesthetic.

- **Target Audience:** Clearly define your target customer base and tailor your marketing efforts accordingly. Understand their needs, preferences, and pain points to create messaging that resonates with them.
- **Marketing Channels:** Utilize a variety of marketing channels to reach your target audience. This could include online advertising, social media, local print publications, community events, and partnerships with local businesses.
- **Promotional Offers:** Offer special promotions and discounts to attract new customers and incentivize repeat business. Consider loyalty programs, referral bonuses, or discounted wash-and-fold services during off-peak hours.
- **Customer Service:** Provide exceptional customer service to build a loyal following. Train your staff to be friendly, helpful, and responsive to customer needs. Address any complaints or issues promptly and professionally.
- **Online Presence:** Create a professional website and social media profiles for your laundromat. Use these platforms to showcase your services, share promotions, and engage with customers.

Remember, your marketing and branding strategy should be an ongoing effort. Continuously evaluate its effectiveness, track key metrics, and adapt your approach as needed to ensure you're reaching your target audience and achieving your desired results.

2.5 Creating a Pricing Structure for Your Services

Determining the right pricing structure for your laundromat services is a critical step in your business plan. Your prices should be competitive, cover your costs, and generate a profit.

Here are some factors to consider when setting your prices:

- **Local Competition:** Research the prices charged by other laundromats in your area. Your prices should be in line with the market, but you can differentiate yourself by offering additional services or amenities.
- **Costs:** Calculate your operating costs, including rent, utilities, payroll, maintenance, and supplies. Your prices should cover these costs and leave room for profit.
- **Target Audience:** Consider the income level and price sensitivity of your target customers. If you're targeting budget-conscious individuals, you may need to offer lower prices or special discounts.
- **Value Proposition:** If you're offering additional services like wash-and-fold or dry cleaning, you can charge a premium for the added convenience.
- **Pricing Strategies:** Consider various pricing strategies, such as tiered pricing (different prices for different machine sizes), time-of-day pricing (lower prices during off-peak hours), or

bundled pricing (offering discounts for multiple services).

Remember to regularly review and adjust your pricing as needed to remain competitive and profitable.

2.6 Writing a Comprehensive Business Plan

Now that you've covered the key elements of your laundromat business plan, it's time to compile everything into a comprehensive document. A well-written business plan is essential for securing funding and guiding your business decisions.

Here's a suggested outline for your laundromat business plan:

1. **Executive Summary:** A concise overview of your business, including your mission, vision, target market, and financial projections.
2. **Company Description:** Detailed information about your laundromat, including its legal structure, ownership, location, and services offered.
3. **Market Analysis:** An in-depth analysis of your target market, competition, and industry trends.
4. **Marketing and Sales Strategy:** Your plan for attracting and retaining customers, including your branding, advertising, and promotional strategies.
5. **Management and Operations:** An overview of your management team, staffing plan, and day-to-day operations.

6. **Financial Projections:** Detailed financial forecasts, including startup costs, revenue projections, expense estimates, and break-even analysis.
7. **Funding Request:** If you're seeking funding, outline your funding needs and how you plan to use the funds.
8. **Appendix:** Include any supporting documents, such as market research data, resumes of key team members, and letters of intent from potential investors.

Your business plan should be clear, concise, and well-organized. Use professional language and avoid jargon. Support your claims with data and evidence. Most importantly, ensure your business plan is realistic and achievable.

2.7 Securing Funding and Investment (Even with Limited Capital)

Securing funding is a critical step in launching your laundromat business. Even if you have limited capital, there are various funding options available to you.

Here are some potential sources of funding:

1. **Personal Savings:** If you have savings, this is often the easiest and most accessible source of funding.
2. **Friends and Family:** Consider approaching friends and family members who might be willing to invest in your business. Be sure to

formalize any loan agreements to avoid misunderstandings.
3. **Small Business Loans:** Many banks and credit unions offer small business loans to entrepreneurs. Prepare a strong business plan and financial projections to increase your chances of approval.
4. **Equipment Financing:** Some equipment suppliers offer financing options, allowing you to spread out the cost of purchasing washers, dryers, and other equipment.
5. **Government Grants and Loans:** Research government programs that offer grants or loans to small businesses. These programs often have specific eligibility requirements.
6. **Crowdfunding:** Platforms like Kickstarter and Indiegogo allow you to raise funds from a large number of people who believe in your business idea.
7. **Angel Investors:** Angel investors are individuals who invest in early-stage businesses in exchange for equity. They can provide not only funding but also valuable mentorship and guidance.
8. **Venture Capital:** Venture capital firms invest in high-growth potential businesses. This option is typically more suitable for established businesses with a proven track record.

When seeking funding, be prepared to present your business plan, financial projections, and a compelling pitch that highlights the potential of your laundromat. Be transparent about your financial situation and demonstrate your commitment to the success of your business.

Remember, securing funding is not just about the money. It's also about finding the right partners who share your vision and can provide valuable support and resources.

Chapter 3

Finding the Perfect Location – Where Laundry Dreams Take Root

Welcome back to our laundromat adventure! In this chapter, we embark on a crucial quest: finding the perfect location for your laundry business. Imagine this as a real estate treasure hunt, where the prize is a thriving hub of cleanliness and community.

The location of your laundromat can make or break its success. It's the foundation upon which your entire business will be built, influencing everything from your customer base to your operating costs. Choose wisely, and you'll create a convenient haven for laundry-goers; choose poorly, and you could face a constant uphill battle.

But fear not! In this chapter, we'll guide you through the entire process of finding the ideal laundromat location. We'll explore factors like evaluating potential sites, analyzing demographics and foot traffic, negotiating lease terms, obtaining permits and licenses, understanding zoning regulations, designing an efficient layout, and ensuring accessibility and safety for your customers.

So, grab your detective hat and magnifying glass, and let's embark on this exciting journey to uncover the perfect spot for your laundromat dreams to take root.

3.1 Evaluating Ideal Laundromat Locations

The first step in finding the perfect location is to define what "ideal" means for your specific laundromat. This involves considering several factors that align with your business goals and target audience.

Here are some key aspects to consider when evaluating potential laundromat locations:

- **Visibility and Accessibility:** Choose a location that is easily visible from the street and has ample parking. Ensure it's accessible for pedestrians and individuals with disabilities. A corner lot or a space with large windows can significantly enhance visibility.
- **Proximity to Target Market:** Consider the demographics of your ideal customers. Are you targeting students, families, or busy professionals? Choose a location that is conveniently located near their homes, workplaces, or other frequently visited areas.
- **Competition:** While some competition is healthy, too much can saturate the market and make it difficult to attract customers. Analyze the density of existing laundromats in the area and assess their strengths and weaknesses.
- **Size and Layout:** The size and layout of the space should accommodate your planned equipment, amenities, and customer flow. Ensure there's enough room for washers, dryers, folding tables, seating areas, and any additional services you intend to offer.

- **Safety and Security:** Prioritize safety by selecting a well-lit location with low crime rates. Consider installing security cameras and alarms to deter theft and vandalism.
- **Zoning and Regulations:** Ensure the location is zoned for commercial use and complies with local regulations regarding laundromats. Check for any restrictions on signage, operating hours, or noise levels.
- **Accessibility to Utilities:** Verify that the location has adequate access to water, electricity, and gas lines to support the operation of your laundromat.

By carefully evaluating these factors, you can narrow down your search and identify potential locations that align with your business goals and vision.

3.2 Analyzing Demographics and Foot Traffic

Once you've identified potential locations, it's time to delve deeper into the demographics of the surrounding area and assess the foot traffic. This data will provide valuable insights into the potential customer base and the demand for laundromat services in the area.

Here's how to analyze demographics and foot traffic:

- **Demographic Data:** Utilize online resources like the U.S. Census Bureau or local government websites to gather demographic data about the area. Look for information on population density, age distribution, income levels,

household size, and other relevant factors. This data will help you determine if the area aligns with your target market.
- **Foot Traffic Analysis:** Observe the foot traffic in the area at different times of the day and week. Note the types of businesses nearby, the density of residential areas, and the presence of public transportation. High foot traffic, especially near apartment buildings, college campuses, or busy commercial areas, can indicate a strong demand for laundromat services.
- **Competition Analysis:** Assess the proximity and offerings of competing laundromats in the area. Are they well-maintained and offer a wide range of services? Are their prices competitive? Understanding your competition will help you differentiate your laundromat and attract customers.
- **Online Tools:** Utilize online tools like Google My Business or Yelp to gather insights into customer reviews and ratings of existing laundromats in the area. This can give you valuable feedback on what customers like and dislike about their current laundry options.

By analyzing demographics and foot traffic, you can gain a deeper understanding of the potential demand for your laundromat and make informed decisions about your location.

3.3 Negotiating Lease Terms and Agreements

Once you've found a promising location, it's time to negotiate the lease terms and agreements with the landlord. This is a critical step that can significantly impact your monthly expenses and overall profitability.

Here are some key points to consider when negotiating a laundromat lease:

- **Lease Term:** Negotiate a lease term that provides you with enough time to establish your business and generate a return on your investment. A typical lease term for a laundromat is five to ten years.
- **Rent:** The rent should be affordable and aligned with your financial projections. Consider negotiating a lower base rent with a percentage of your gross sales as additional rent.
- **Maintenance and Repairs:** Clearly define the responsibilities of the landlord and tenant regarding maintenance and repairs. Ideally, the landlord should be responsible for major structural repairs, while you handle routine maintenance.
- **Renewal Options:** Negotiate the option to renew your lease at the end of the term. This will give you the flexibility to continue operating your business if it's successful.
- **Exclusivity Clause:** Consider negotiating an exclusivity clause that prevents the landlord

from leasing space to another laundromat in the same building or complex.
- **Signage:** Ensure you have the right to display signage for your laundromat.
- **Utilities:** Clarify who is responsible for paying for utilities like water, electricity, and gas.
- **Insurance:** Determine the insurance requirements for the lease and ensure you have adequate coverage for your business.

It's advisable to consult with a real estate attorney or a commercial leasing specialist to help you negotiate the best possible lease terms for your laundromat.

3.4 Obtaining Necessary Permits and Licenses

Operating a laundromat requires obtaining various permits and licenses to ensure compliance with local and state regulations. The specific requirements vary depending on your location, but some common permits and licenses include:

- **Business License:** A general business license is required to operate any business, including a laundromat.
- **Sales Tax Permit:** If you plan to sell laundry products or offer wash-and-fold services, you'll likely need a sales tax permit.
- **Health Permit:** A health permit ensures that your laundromat meets sanitation and hygiene standards.
- **Fire Safety Permit:** A fire safety permit verifies that your laundromat complies with fire safety regulations.

- **Environmental Permit:** Depending on your location and the type of equipment you use, you may need an environmental permit to address wastewater disposal and other environmental concerns.
- **Sign Permit:** If you plan to display signage for your laundromat, you'll need a sign permit.

The process for obtaining permits and licenses can be time-consuming and complex. It's advisable to start the process early and seek assistance from local government agencies or business development centers to ensure you have all the necessary documentation.

3.5 Understanding Zoning Regulations

Zoning regulations dictate how land can be used in a specific area. Before finalizing your laundromat location, it's crucial to understand the zoning regulations in your chosen area to ensure it's permissible to operate a laundromat there.

Zoning regulations can vary widely depending on the municipality. Some areas may have specific zones designated for commercial use, while others may have restrictions on the types of businesses allowed in certain neighborhoods.

Here's what to consider regarding zoning regulations:

- **Permitted Use:** Verify that the zoning classification of the property allows for the operation of a laundromat.
- **Parking Requirements:** Check if there are any specific parking requirements for commercial businesses in the area.

- **Signage Restrictions:** Some areas may have limitations on the size, type, or placement of signage.
- **Noise Restrictions:** Laundromats can generate noise from machines and customer activity. Ensure that the noise levels comply with local regulations, especially if the laundromat is located near residential areas.
- **Environmental Regulations:** Inquire about any environmental regulations that may apply to your laundromat, such as restrictions on wastewater disposal or chemical usage.

To avoid any surprises or legal issues, it's crucial to consult with local zoning officials or a real estate attorney who specializes in commercial zoning. They can help you understand the regulations and ensure your laundromat complies with all applicable laws.

3.6 Designing Your Laundromat Layout for Efficiency

The layout of your laundromat plays a crucial role in its overall efficiency, functionality, and customer experience. A well-designed layout can optimize workflow, maximize space utilization, and create a welcoming environment for your customers.

Here are some key considerations for designing an efficient laundromat layout:

- **Workflow:** Design the layout to facilitate a smooth flow of customer traffic. Place the washers and dryers in a logical sequence, with ample space for customers to maneuver carts or baskets.

Accessibility: Ensure that all areas of the laundromat are easily accessible for individuals with disabilities, including those using wheelchairs or walkers. Provide ample space between machines and ensure clear pathways.

- **Equipment Placement:** Strategically place washers and dryers to optimize space and efficiency. Consider placing larger capacity machines towards the back, encouraging customers to venture further into your space. Position smaller, quick-cycle machines near the front for convenience.
- **Folding Areas:** Allocate ample space for folding tables and ensure they are conveniently located near the dryers. Consider installing counters or shelves above the folding tables for additional storage.
- **Seating:** Provide comfortable seating areas for customers waiting for their laundry. Consider incorporating a mix of individual chairs, benches, and booths to accommodate different group sizes.
- **Amenities:** Enhance the customer experience by offering additional amenities like vending machines for snacks and drinks, change machines, soap dispensers, and free Wi-Fi. If space allows, consider adding a children's play area or a television.

- **Lighting:** Ensure adequate lighting throughout the laundromat. Use a combination of natural and artificial lighting to create a bright and inviting atmosphere.
- **Ventilation:** Proper ventilation is essential to maintain a comfortable environment and prevent the buildup of humidity and odors. Install exhaust fans and ensure proper airflow throughout the space.
- **Signage:** Use clear and concise signage to guide customers through the laundromat. Label machines with instructions, pricing information, and any special features. Consider using visual cues like arrows or floor markings to direct traffic flow.
- **Aesthetics:** Create an appealing and visually pleasing environment. Use a cohesive color scheme, incorporate artwork or murals, and maintain a clean and organized space. A welcoming atmosphere can encourage customers to return and recommend your laundromat to others.

Consider consulting with an architect or interior designer who specializes in commercial spaces to help you create a functional and aesthetically pleasing layout. They can provide valuable insights and ensure your laundromat is designed for optimal efficiency and customer satisfaction.

3.7 Ensuring Accessibility and Safety for Customers

Creating a safe and accessible environment for your customers is paramount for the success of your laundromat. This involves adhering to regulations, implementing safety measures, and considering the needs of all customers, including those with disabilities.

Here's how to ensure accessibility and safety for your customers:

- **Accessibility:** Comply with the Americans with Disabilities Act (ADA) by ensuring that your laundromat is accessible to individuals with disabilities. This includes providing ramps, wide doorways, accessible restrooms, and lowered counters or machines. Consider offering assistance to customers with disabilities, such as help loading and unloading machines.
- **Safety Measures:** Install security cameras, alarms, and adequate lighting to deter theft and vandalism. Ensure that all equipment is properly maintained and inspected regularly for safety hazards. Post clear safety guidelines and instructions for using machines and chemicals.
- **Emergency Preparedness:** Develop an emergency preparedness plan that includes procedures for handling fires, floods, power outages, and other potential hazards. Train

your staff on emergency protocols and ensure that fire extinguishers and first-aid kits are readily available.
- **Cleanliness and Hygiene:** Maintain high standards of cleanliness and hygiene throughout your laundromat. Regularly clean and disinfect machines, floors, restrooms, and common areas. Provide hand sanitizers and encourage customers to practice good hygiene.
- **Clear Signage:** Post clear and visible signage throughout your laundromat to indicate emergency exits, safety procedures, and instructions for using machines and chemicals.
- **Customer Feedback:** Encourage customers to provide feedback on their experience and address any concerns promptly. This will help you identify and address any potential safety or accessibility issues.

By prioritizing accessibility and safety, you can create a welcoming and inclusive environment for all customers, fostering a positive reputation and building long-term loyalty.

Chapter 4

Equipping Your Laundromat – Building the Heart of Your Laundry Haven

Welcome back to our laundromat odyssey! In this chapter, we'll dive into the exciting process of equipping your laundromat, transforming your chosen space into a fully functional and inviting laundry haven. Think of it as outfitting your laundry empire with the tools, technology, and comforts that will make your customers' experience seamless and enjoyable.

Equipping your laundromat is a significant investment, but it's also a crucial one. The right equipment will not only attract customers but also ensure the smooth operation of your business, maximize efficiency, and contribute to your long-term profitability. In this chapter, we'll cover everything you need to know to make informed decisions about choosing washers and dryers, selecting additional equipment like vending machines and change machines, budgeting for maintenance and repairs, finding reliable suppliers, implementing energy-efficient systems, and creating a comfortable and secure atmosphere for your customers.

So, let's roll up our sleeves and dive into the world of laundry equipment, exploring the latest innovations, industry trends, and essential considerations for outfitting your laundromat for success.

4.1 Choosing the Right Washers and Dryers

The heart and soul of any laundromat are its washers and dryers. These machines are the workhorses of your business, churning out clean clothes day in and day out. Choosing the right washers and dryers is essential for providing quality service, ensuring customer satisfaction, and maximizing your return on investment.

Here are some key factors to consider when choosing washers and dryers for your laundromat:

- **Capacity:** Determine the size and capacity of machines you need based on your anticipated customer volume and the types of laundry they are likely to bring in. Offer a variety of machine sizes to accommodate different needs, from small loads to bulky items like comforters and blankets.
- **Efficiency:** Invest in energy-efficient washers and dryers to reduce your operating costs and minimize your environmental impact. Look for models with high water efficiency ratings (WF) and energy efficiency ratings (EE).
- **Durability and Reliability:** Laundromat machines are used heavily, so it's crucial to choose durable and reliable models that can withstand constant use. Look for brands with a reputation for quality and longevity.

- **Features:** Consider additional features like multiple cycle options, sanitization settings, automatic detergent dispensers, and high-spin speeds for faster drying times. These features can enhance the customer experience and differentiate your laundromat from the competition.
- **Price:** Washers and dryers come in a wide range of prices, so it's important to set a budget and prioritize your needs. While it might be tempting to go for the cheapest options, remember that investing in quality equipment will save you money in the long run through reduced maintenance and repair costs.
- **Warranty and Service:** Choose brands that offer comprehensive warranties and reliable service to ensure that your machines are always up and running.
- **Brand Reputation:** Research different brands and their reputation in the industry. Talk to other laundromat owners to get their feedback and recommendations.

Here are some popular brands of commercial laundry equipment:

- **Speed Queen:** Known for their durability, reliability, and long lifespan.
- **Maytag Commercial Laundry:** Offers a wide range of energy-efficient and technologically advanced machines.
- **Whirlpool Commercial Laundry:** Provides reliable and easy-to-use machines with a variety of features.

- **Dexter Laundry:** Offers a comprehensive selection of washers, dryers, and other laundry equipment.
- **Electrolux Professional:** Known for their innovative and eco-friendly laundry solutions.

When choosing washers and dryers, don't be afraid to mix and match brands and models to create a diverse selection that caters to different customer needs and budgets.

4.2 Selecting Additional Equipment

In addition to washers and dryers, several other pieces of equipment are essential for a fully functional laundromat. These include:

- **Change Machines:** Provide customers with a convenient way to convert bills into coins for using the machines. Consider offering a bill breaker that dispenses both coins and smaller bills for added convenience.
- **Vending Machines:** Offer snacks, drinks, laundry supplies, and other essentials to enhance the customer experience and generate additional revenue.
- **Folding Tables:** Provide ample space for customers to fold their laundry. Ensure the tables are sturdy, clean, and conveniently located near the dryers.
- **Carts or Baskets:** Offer carts or baskets for customers to transport their laundry from the washers to the dryers and folding tables. This can be a valuable amenity, especially for customers with large loads.

- **Soap Dispensers:** Consider installing automatic soap dispensers for added convenience and to encourage customers to use the correct amount of detergent.
- **Security Cameras:** Install security cameras to deter theft, vandalism, and other security issues. Ensure cameras are strategically placed to monitor all areas of the laundromat.
- **Alarms:** Consider installing an alarm system to further enhance security and protect your investment.
- **Water Heating System:** If you're not using gas-powered dryers, you'll need a water heating system to provide hot water for the washers.
- **Utility Sinks:** Provide utility sinks for customers to pre-treat stains or rinse out items.
- **Trash Cans and Recycling Bins:** Encourage responsible waste disposal by providing ample trash cans and recycling bins throughout the laundromat.

The specific equipment you choose will depend on your budget, space limitations, and the services you offer.

4.3 Budgeting for Maintenance and Repairs

Maintaining your laundromat equipment is essential for ensuring its longevity, reliability, and optimal performance. Unexpected breakdowns can disrupt your business and lead to frustrated customers. Therefore, it's crucial to budget for regular maintenance and repairs.

Here's how to budget for maintenance and repairs:

- **Regular Maintenance:** Schedule regular maintenance for your washers, dryers, and other equipment. This may include cleaning lint traps, inspecting hoses and belts, and lubricating moving parts. Refer to the manufacturer's instructions for recommended maintenance schedules.
- **Preventive Maintenance:** Invest in preventive maintenance to identify and address potential issues before they escalate into major repairs. This could involve regular inspections by a qualified technician, replacement of worn-out parts, and software updates.
- **Repair Fund:** Set aside a portion of your revenue each month to create a repair fund. This fund will cover unexpected repairs and ensure you have the resources to address any equipment malfunctions promptly.
- **Warranty Coverage:** Utilize warranty coverage for repairs that fall under the manufacturer's warranty. Keep track of warranty expiration dates and contact the manufacturer or supplier for assistance with covered repairs.
- **Service Contracts:** Consider purchasing service contracts for your equipment. These contracts often include preventive maintenance and priority service for repairs, providing peace of mind and minimizing downtime.

By proactively budgeting for maintenance and repairs, you can avoid costly surprises and ensure the smooth operation of your laundromat.

4.4 Finding Reliable Suppliers and Vendors

Establishing relationships with reliable suppliers and vendors is essential for securing quality equipment, obtaining competitive prices, and ensuring timely delivery and service.

Here's how to find reliable suppliers and vendors:

- **Research:** Research different suppliers and vendors in your area and compare their offerings, prices, and reputation. Read online reviews, talk to other laundromat owners, and attend industry trade shows to gather information.
- **Request Quotes:** Request quotes from multiple suppliers for the equipment you need. Compare prices, warranties, delivery times, and service agreements.
- **Check References:** Ask suppliers for references from other laundromat owners and contact them to inquire about their experience with the supplier.
- **Negotiate:** Don't be afraid to negotiate prices and terms with suppliers. Bulk purchases or long-term contracts may entitle you to discounts.
- **Build Relationships:** Establish strong relationships with your suppliers and vendors.

Communicate your needs clearly, pay invoices on time, and provide feedback on their products and services. This can lead to better deals, priority service, and access to new products and technologies.

By building a network of reliable suppliers and vendors, you can ensure that your laundromat is equipped with quality products and receives prompt and efficient service.

4.5 Installing Energy-Efficient Systems

Energy costs can be a significant expense for laundromats. However, by implementing energy-efficient systems, you can significantly reduce your operating costs and minimize your environmental impact.

Here are some energy-saving strategies for your laundromat:

- **Energy-Efficient Machines:** Invest in ENERGY STAR certified washers and dryers. These machines use less water and electricity, leading to substantial savings over time.
- **High-Spin Washers:** High-spin washers extract more water from clothes during the wash cycle, reducing drying times and energy consumption.
- **Water Recycling Systems:** Consider installing a water recycling system that filters and reuses wastewater for certain laundry cycles. This can

significantly reduce your water consumption and lower your utility bills.
- **Heat Recovery Systems:** Heat recovery systems capture waste heat from dryers and use it to preheat incoming water for washers, reducing the energy needed to heat water.
- **LED Lighting:** Replace traditional light bulbs with energy-efficient LED lighting. LEDs use less energy and last longer, resulting in long-term savings.
- **Occupancy Sensors:** Install occupancy sensors to turn off lights and other equipment when not in use, further reducing energy consumption.

Regular Maintenance: Ensure that all equipment is properly maintained and calibrated for optimal energy efficiency.

- **Solar Panels:** If feasible, consider installing solar panels to generate renewable energy for your laundromat. This can significantly reduce your reliance on the grid and lower your energy costs in the long run.

By implementing these energy-efficient systems and practices, you can not only save money but also contribute to a greener and more sustainable future. Additionally, promoting your laundromat as eco-friendly can attract environmentally conscious customers and enhance your brand image.

4.6 Implementing Security Measures

Security is a top priority for any laundromat owner. Protecting your investment, ensuring the safety of your customers, and deterring theft and vandalism are crucial for the smooth operation of your business.

Here are some key security measures to implement in your laundromat:

- **Security Cameras:** Install high-resolution security cameras both inside and outside your laundromat. Ensure they cover all areas, including entrances, exits, laundry areas, folding tables, and parking lots. Consider using cameras with remote viewing capabilities so you can monitor your laundromat from anywhere.
- **Alarm Systems:** Install a comprehensive alarm system that includes door and window sensors, motion detectors, and a loud siren. Connect the alarm system to a central monitoring station for 24/7 surveillance.
- **Access Control:** Restrict access to certain areas of your laundromat, such as the office or storage room, by using keycard systems or other access control measures. This can prevent unauthorized entry and protect valuable assets.
- **Lighting:** Ensure adequate lighting both inside and outside your laundromat. Well-lit areas deter criminal activity and create a sense of safety for your customers.

- **Security Personnel:** Consider hiring security personnel, especially if your laundromat is open 24/7 or located in a high-crime area. Security personnel can patrol the premises, monitor surveillance footage, and respond to any incidents.
- **Cash Handling Procedures:** Implement secure cash handling procedures to minimize the risk of theft. Limit the amount of cash on hand, use a drop safe, and regularly deposit cash in the bank.
- **Employee Training:** Train your staff on security protocols, including how to handle suspicious activity, respond to emergencies, and de-escalate conflicts.
- **Customer Awareness:** Encourage customers to be vigilant about their belongings and report any suspicious activity to staff. Post signs reminding customers to keep an eye on their valuables.

By implementing these security measures, you can create a safe and secure environment for your customers and employees, deterring criminal activity and protecting your investment.

4.7 Creating a Comfortable and Inviting Atmosphere

The atmosphere of your laundromat plays a significant role in attracting and retaining customers. A comfortable and inviting environment can make the laundry experience more enjoyable, encouraging customers to return and recommend your business to others.

Here are some tips for creating a welcoming atmosphere in your laundromat:

- **Cleanliness:** Maintain a high standard of cleanliness throughout your laundromat. Regularly clean and disinfect machines, floors, restrooms, and common areas. A clean environment not only enhances the customer experience but also promotes hygiene and safety.
- **Lighting:** Use a combination of natural and artificial lighting to create a bright and inviting atmosphere. Avoid harsh fluorescent lighting, which can be unflattering and create a sterile feel. Consider using warm-toned LED lights or natural light from windows.
- **Color Scheme:** Choose a color scheme that is calming, inviting, and promotes relaxation. Avoid overly bright or harsh colors, which can be overwhelming or distracting. Consider using neutral tones like white, beige, or gray, with pops of color from artwork or decorative elements.
- **Seating:** Provide comfortable seating options for customers waiting for their laundry. Offer a variety of seating options, such as individual chairs, benches, and booths, to accommodate different group sizes and preferences.
- **Amenities:** Offer amenities like free Wi-Fi, vending machines, charging stations, and

televisions to make the wait more enjoyable for customers. If space allows, consider adding a children's play area or a coffee bar.
- **Music and Entertainment:** Play calming music or ambient sounds to create a relaxing atmosphere. Consider installing televisions or offering reading materials to keep customers entertained while they wait.
- **Temperature Control:** Ensure the temperature in your laundromat is comfortable year-round. Install air conditioning for the summer and heating for the winter.
- **Greenery:** Add plants or flowers to your laundromat to bring a touch of nature indoors and create a more inviting atmosphere.
- **Artwork and Décor:** Incorporate artwork, murals, or other decorative elements to add personality and visual interest to your laundromat.

By paying attention to these details and creating a comfortable and inviting atmosphere, you can turn your laundromat into a welcoming space where customers feel valued and enjoy spending time.

Chapter 5

Launching Your Laundromat – The Grand Unveiling of Your Laundry Haven

Welcome to the most exhilarating chapter of our laundromat journey: the grand opening! This is where your meticulous planning, hard work, and entrepreneurial spirit culminate in the unveiling of your laundry haven to the world.

Launching a laundromat is a momentous occasion, filled with both excitement and anticipation. It's a chance to showcase your unique vision, attract eager customers, and establish your business as a valuable asset to the community. But it also requires careful planning, strategic marketing, and a keen understanding of your target audience.

In this chapter, we'll guide you through the entire process of launching your laundromat, from developing a grand opening marketing plan to creating a memorable launch event, implementing effective pricing strategies, building customer loyalty programs, utilizing social media and online marketing, partnering with local businesses, and tracking key performance indicators (KPIs). By the end of this chapter, you'll be equipped with the knowledge and tools to make your laundromat launch a resounding success.

So, let's roll out the red carpet, hang the balloons, and prepare to welcome the community to your sparkling new laundry destination.

5.1 Developing a Grand Opening Marketing Plan

A grand opening marketing plan is your blueprint for generating buzz, attracting customers, and creating a lasting first impression. It's a comprehensive strategy that combines various marketing channels and tactics to maximize your reach and impact.

Here are some key elements of a successful grand opening marketing plan:

- **Target Audience:** Identify your target customer base and tailor your marketing messages accordingly. Understand their needs, preferences, and pain points to create compelling content that resonates with them.
- **Messaging:** Craft clear, concise, and engaging messaging that highlights the unique features and benefits of your laundromat. Emphasize convenience, affordability, cleanliness, and any additional services or amenities you offer.
- **Marketing Channels:** Utilize a diverse range of marketing channels to reach your target audience. This could include online advertising (Google Ads, social media ads), local print publications (newspapers, flyers), community events (festivals, fairs), partnerships with local

businesses (dry cleaners, hair salons), and direct mail campaigns.
- **Timeline:** Create a detailed timeline for your marketing efforts, starting several weeks before your grand opening. Gradually increase the intensity of your marketing as the opening date approaches, creating a sense of anticipation and excitement.
- **Budget:** Allocate a realistic budget for your marketing efforts. Consider the cost of advertising, printing materials, promotional items, and any paid partnerships or sponsorships.
- **Tracking and Measurement:** Implement tracking mechanisms to measure the effectiveness of your marketing campaigns. Track website traffic, social media engagement, customer inquiries, and any promotional codes or discounts you offer. This data will help you assess the success of your marketing efforts and make adjustments as needed.

By developing a well-structured and targeted marketing plan, you can generate buzz, attract customers, and ensure a successful grand opening for your laundromat.

5.2 Creating a Memorable Launch Event

Your grand opening event is an opportunity to make a lasting impression on your community and kickstart your business with a bang. It's a chance to showcase your laundromat's unique features, create a festive atmosphere, and build relationships with potential customers.

Here are some ideas for creating a memorable launch event:

- **Theme:** Choose a theme that aligns with your brand identity and resonates with your target audience. This could be a "clean clothes carnival," a "laundry luau," or a "fresh start fiesta."
- **Activities:** Plan engaging activities that appeal to all ages, such as face painting, balloon animals, raffles, games, or live music. Consider partnering with local businesses or vendors to offer additional attractions, like food trucks or pop-up shops.
- **Promotions:** Offer special discounts, free washes, or other incentives to entice customers to try your laundromat during the grand opening. Consider partnering with local businesses to offer cross-promotions or discounts.
- **Community Involvement:** Invite local officials, community leaders, and media representatives to your event. Partner with local charities or organizations to give back to the community and generate positive publicity.
- **Decorations:** Decorate your laundromat with festive decorations that align with your theme. Use balloons, streamers, banners, and signage to create a vibrant and welcoming atmosphere.

- **Refreshments:** Offer complimentary refreshments like snacks, drinks, or coffee to your guests. This can create a more relaxed and enjoyable experience for everyone.
- **Photo Opportunities:** Create photo opportunities for customers to share on social media. This could include a themed photo booth, a backdrop with your laundromat's logo, or fun props related to laundry.
- **Follow-up:** After the event, follow up with attendees by sending thank-you emails or offering special discounts for their next visit. This will help to build customer loyalty and encourage repeat business.

By creating a memorable launch event, you can generate positive word-of-mouth, build brand awareness, and attract a loyal customer base from day one.

5.3 Implementing Effective Pricing Strategies

Pricing your laundromat services strategically is essential for attracting customers, covering your costs, and generating a profit. It requires careful consideration of various factors, including your operating costs, competition, target audience, and the value proposition of your services.

Here are some effective pricing strategies for laundromats:

- **Tiered Pricing:** Offer different prices for different machine sizes or wash cycles. This

allows customers to choose the option that best suits their needs and budget.
- **Time-of-Day Pricing:** Offer lower prices during off-peak hours to incentivize customers to visit during less busy times. This can help to distribute demand more evenly throughout the day and avoid overcrowding during peak hours.
- **Bundled Pricing:** Offer discounts or package deals for customers who use multiple services, such as wash-and-fold and dry cleaning. This can encourage customers to try new services and increase your average transaction value.
- **Loyalty Programs:** Reward loyal customers with discounts, free washes, or other incentives. This can help to build customer retention and encourage repeat business.
- **Membership Programs:** Offer a membership program that provides customers with exclusive benefits, such as discounted rates, priority access to machines, or free laundry bags. This can create a sense of exclusivity and incentivize customers to choose your laundromat over competitors.
- **Dynamic Pricing:** Consider using dynamic pricing, where prices fluctuate based on demand, time of day, or other factors. This can help you maximize revenue during peak hours and attract customers during slower periods with lower prices.
- **Value-Based Pricing:** If your laundromat offers premium services or amenities, consider value-

based pricing, where you charge a premium for the added value and convenience you provide.

When setting your prices, be sure to research your local market and understand the pricing strategies of your competitors. Your prices should be competitive, but also reflect the unique value proposition of your laundromat.

5.4 Building Customer Loyalty Programs

Customer loyalty is the lifeblood of any successful business, and laundromats are no exception. Building a loyal customer base ensures a steady stream of revenue, positive word-of-mouth marketing, and a thriving community around your brand.

Here are some effective strategies for building customer loyalty in your laundromat:

- **Loyalty Programs:** Implement a loyalty program that rewards customers for their repeat business. This could involve offering discounts, free washes, or exclusive perks after a certain number of visits or spending a specific amount.
- **Personalized Service:** Train your staff to provide friendly, helpful, and personalized service to every customer. Remember names, offer assistance with machines, and go the extra mile to make customers feel valued.
- **Feedback and Reviews:** Encourage customers to leave feedback and reviews on platforms like Google My Business or Yelp. Respond to all

reviews, both positive and negative, to show that you value customer feedback and are committed to improving your services.
- **Special Events and Promotions:** Host special events or promotions throughout the year to engage customers and show appreciation for their loyalty. This could include themed laundry days, holiday celebrations, or partnerships with local businesses.
- **Communication:** Keep customers informed about new services, promotions, or events through email newsletters, social media posts, or in-store signage. Consider sending personalized birthday greetings or special offers to loyal customers.
- **Community Involvement:** Get involved in your local community by sponsoring events, donating to charities, or partnering with local organizations. This can help you build a positive reputation and foster goodwill among your customers.
- **Going the Extra Mile:** Offer additional services or amenities that go beyond the basics. This could include free Wi-Fi, charging stations, coffee, snacks, or even a children's play area.

By implementing these strategies, you can create a loyal customer base that sees your laundromat as more than just a place to do laundry. It becomes a destination, a community hub, and a place where they feel valued and appreciated.

5.5 Utilizing Social Media and Online Marketing

In today's digital age, social media and online marketing are essential tools for reaching your target audience and promoting your laundromat. These platforms offer a cost-effective way to connect with potential customers, build brand awareness, and drive traffic to your business.

Here's how to leverage social media and online marketing for your laundromat:

- **Social Media Presence:** Create profiles on relevant social media platforms like Facebook, Instagram, and Twitter. Share engaging content like photos of your laundromat, customer testimonials, laundry tips, and promotions. Use relevant hashtags to reach a wider audience.
- **Online Advertising:** Run targeted online ads on platforms like Google Ads and social media to reach potential customers in your area. Use keywords relevant to your services, such as "laundromat near me," "wash and fold," or "coin laundry."
- **Local SEO:** Optimize your website and online listings (Google My Business, Yelp, etc.) for local search. This will ensure that your laundromat appears in search results when people search for laundry services in your area.
- **Content Marketing:** Create informative and engaging content, such as blog posts, videos, or

infographics, on topics related to laundry care, stain removal, or eco-friendly practices. Share this content on your website and social media channels to attract potential customers and position yourself as a laundry expert.
- **Email Marketing:** Collect customer email addresses and send regular newsletters with promotions, updates, and laundry tips. Offer incentives for signing up, such as a discount on their first wash or a free laundry bag.
- **Online Reviews:** Encourage customers to leave reviews on platforms like Google My Business or Yelp. Respond to all reviews, both positive and negative, to show that you value customer feedback and are committed to improving your services.
- **Partnerships and Collaborations:** Partner with local businesses or influencers to cross-promote your services. This could involve offering discounts to their customers or collaborating on social media campaigns.
- **Website:** Create a user-friendly website that showcases your services, pricing, location, and contact information. Include a booking system for wash-and-fold services or an online payment option for added convenience.

By utilizing social media and online marketing strategically, you can effectively reach your target audience, build brand awareness, and drive traffic to your laundromat.

5.6 Partnering with Local Businesses

Partnering with local businesses is a mutually beneficial strategy that can help you expand your reach, attract new customers, and build a stronger presence in your community.

Here are some ideas for partnering with local businesses:

- **Cross-Promotions:** Offer discounts or special offers to customers of partnering businesses, and vice-versa. For example, you could partner with a nearby coffee shop to offer a discount on coffee to your laundromat customers, and they could offer a discount on laundry services to their coffee shop customers.
- **Joint Events:** Host joint events or promotions with partnering businesses. This could include a "laundry and latte" day where customers receive a discount on both laundry services and coffee, or a "clean clothes and cocktails" night where customers enjoy discounted drinks at a local bar after doing their laundry.
- **Referral Programs:** Create a referral program where customers receive a discount or reward for referring friends and family to your laundromat. Partnering businesses can also participate in the referral program, referring their customers to your laundromat for a mutually beneficial relationship.
- **Community Events:** Participate in community events together, such as local festivals, fairs, or

charity events. This can help you raise awareness for both businesses and build goodwill within the community.
- **Co-Marketing:** Collaborate on marketing campaigns, such as social media contests, joint advertisements, or co-branded merchandise. This can help you reach a wider audience and reinforce your brand message.

By partnering with local businesses, you can tap into their existing customer base, increase your visibility, and build a stronger presence in your community. This can lead to increased foot traffic, brand loyalty, and a thriving business ecosystem.

5.7 Tracking Key Performance Indicators (KPIs)

Tracking key performance indicators (KPIs) is essential for measuring the success of your laundromat launch and identifying areas for improvement. KPIs are quantifiable metrics that provide insights into the performance of your business, allowing you to make data-driven decisions and optimize your operations.

Here are some key KPIs to track for your laundromat launch:

- **Customer Acquisition:** Track the number of new customers acquired during your launch period. This can be measured through sign-ups for loyalty programs, redeemed promotional offers, or customer surveys.

- **Customer Retention:** Measure the percentage of customers who return for repeat business. This can be tracked through loyalty program data, customer surveys, or simply by observing repeat visits.
- **Revenue:** Track your total revenue during the launch period and compare it to your projected figures. This will help you assess the financial performance of your launch and identify any discrepancies.
- **Profitability:** Calculate your profit margin by subtracting your expenses from your revenue. This will give you a clear picture of your financial health and help you identify areas where you can cut costs or increase revenue.
- **Average Transaction Value (ATV):** Calculate the average amount spent by customers per visit. This can be increased by offering bundled services, upselling additional products, or implementing loyalty programs.
- **Customer Satisfaction:** Measure customer satisfaction through surveys, feedback forms, or online reviews. This will help you identify areas where you can improve your services and enhance the customer experience.
- **Social Media Engagement:** Track metrics like likes, shares, comments, and followers on your social media channels. This will help you gauge the effectiveness of your social media marketing efforts.
- **Website Traffic:** Monitor your website traffic, including the number of visitors, page views, and bounce rate. This can help you assess the

effectiveness of your online marketing and identify areas for improvement on your website.

By regularly tracking and analyzing these KPIs, you can gain valuable insights into the performance of your laundromat launch and make informed decisions to optimize your operations, improve customer satisfaction, and drive long-term growth.

Chapter 6

Day-to-Day Laundromat Operations – The Rhythm of Laundry Life

Welcome back, laundrypreneurs! The doors are open, the machines are humming, and customers are flowing in. Now it's time to delve into the heart of your laundromat: its daily operations. This is where the rubber meets the road, where your meticulous planning and preparation translate into the smooth functioning of your business.

Day-to-day operations are the lifeblood of your laundromat. They encompass everything from staffing and inventory management to cleaning procedures, customer service, and technology utilization. This chapter will guide you through the intricacies of managing your laundromat efficiently, ensuring a seamless experience for your customers and a profitable venture for you.

So, let's put on our aprons, grab our cleaning supplies, and immerse ourselves in the rhythm of laundry life.

6.1 Hiring and Training Staff (If Applicable)

If you're running a larger laundromat or offering services like wash-and-fold, you'll likely need to hire staff to help you manage the daily operations. Hiring the right people and providing adequate training is crucial for ensuring excellent customer service, maintaining a clean and organized facility, and upholding your brand's reputation.

Here's a step-by-step guide to hiring and training staff for your laundromat:

1. **Job Descriptions:** Create detailed job descriptions outlining the responsibilities, qualifications, and expectations for each position. Common laundromat roles include attendants, wash-and-fold specialists, and managers.
2. **Recruitment:** Advertise open positions through various channels, such as online job boards, local newspapers, community bulletin boards, and social media. You can also reach out to local employment agencies or vocational schools for potential candidates.
3. **Interviews:** Conduct thorough interviews to assess candidates' experience, skills, and personality. Look for individuals who are friendly, customer-oriented, detail-oriented, and reliable.
4. **Background Checks:** Conduct background checks on potential hires to ensure their suitability for working in a customer-facing environment.
5. **Onboarding:** Provide a comprehensive onboarding process for new hires. This should include an overview of your laundromat's mission, values, and operating procedures.

Introduce them to the team and give them a tour of the facility.

6. **Training:** Develop a comprehensive training program that covers all aspects of the job, including customer service, machine operation and maintenance, cleaning procedures, and safety protocols. Provide hands-on training and shadowing opportunities to ensure new hires are confident and competent in their roles.
7. **Ongoing Training:** Provide ongoing training to keep your staff up-to-date on new products, services, or procedures. Encourage them to share feedback and suggestions for improvement.
8. **Performance Evaluation:** Regularly evaluate your staff's performance and provide constructive feedback. Recognize and reward exceptional performance to boost morale and motivate your team.
9. **Employee Retention:** Create a positive and supportive work environment to foster employee loyalty and reduce turnover. Offer competitive wages, benefits, and opportunities for growth and advancement.

By investing in your staff, you can build a strong and dedicated team that contributes to the success of your laundromat and delivers exceptional service to your customers.

6.2 Managing Inventory and Supplies

Effective inventory management is essential for ensuring that your laundromat always has the necessary supplies on hand to meet customer demand. This includes everything from laundry detergent and fabric softener to laundry bags, hangers, and cleaning supplies.

Here are some tips for managing inventory and supplies in your laundromat:

- **Inventory Tracking:** Keep track of your inventory levels using a spreadsheet or inventory management software. This will help you identify when it's time to reorder supplies and avoid running out of stock.
- **Par Levels:** Establish par levels for each item in your inventory. Par levels are the minimum quantity of a particular item that you should have on hand at all times. This ensures you have enough stock to meet demand without overstocking.
- **Reordering:** Set up a system for reordering supplies when inventory levels reach their par levels. Consider using automated ordering systems or setting up recurring orders with your suppliers to streamline the process.
- **Storage:** Organize your storage area to ensure easy access to supplies and prevent spoilage or damage. Label shelves and bins clearly and keep an inventory list readily available.

- **Stock Rotation:** Practice first-in, first-out (FIFO) stock rotation to ensure that older supplies are used before newer ones. This helps to prevent spoilage and ensures that customers always receive fresh products.
- **Supplier Relationships:** Build strong relationships with your suppliers to ensure reliable delivery and competitive prices. Consider negotiating bulk discounts or setting up automatic reordering for frequently used items.
- **Cost Control:** Regularly review your inventory costs and look for ways to save money. This could involve negotiating better prices with suppliers, switching to more cost-effective products, or reducing waste through better inventory management practices.

By implementing effective inventory management practices, you can ensure that your laundromat always has the necessary supplies on hand to meet customer demand while minimizing waste and controlling costs.

6.3 Implementing Efficient Cleaning Procedures

Maintaining a clean and hygienic environment is paramount for a laundromat. Customers expect a clean and well-maintained facility where they can feel comfortable doing their laundry. Implementing efficient cleaning procedures is essential for upholding your brand's reputation, ensuring customer satisfaction, and complying with health and safety regulations.

Here are some essential cleaning tasks for your laundromat:

- **Washing Machines and Dryers:** Regularly clean and disinfect the interiors and exteriors of all machines. Wipe down control panels, remove lint from traps, and sanitize door seals and handles.
- **Folding Tables:** Clean and disinfect folding tables after each use. Remove any debris or stains and ensure they are dry before the next customer uses them.
- **Floors:** Sweep and mop floors daily, paying special attention to high-traffic areas. Clean up any spills or stains immediately to prevent slips and falls.
- **Restrooms:** Clean and disinfect restrooms multiple times a day. Restock toilet paper, paper towels, soap, and hand sanitizer as needed.
- **Trash Cans and Recycling Bins:** Empty trash cans and recycling bins regularly throughout the day. Keep them clean and free of odors.
- **Vending Machines:** Wipe down vending machines regularly and restock them as needed.
- **Windows and Doors:** Clean windows and doors to maintain a bright and welcoming appearance.

- **Air Vents and Filters:** Clean air vents and filters regularly to ensure proper ventilation and prevent the buildup of dust and allergens.
- **Exterior:** Maintain the cleanliness of the exterior of your laundromat, including the parking lot, sidewalks, and signage.

To ensure efficient cleaning, establish a cleaning schedule that outlines daily, weekly, and monthly tasks. Assign responsibilities to staff members and provide them with the necessary training and supplies.

Consider using environmentally friendly cleaning products to minimize your impact on the environment and appeal to eco-conscious customers.

6.4 Handling Customer Complaints and Issues

No matter how well you run your laundromat, you're bound to encounter customer complaints or issues from time to time. How you handle these situations can significantly impact your reputation and customer loyalty.

Here are some tips for handling customer complaints and issues effectively:

- **Listen Actively:** Listen attentively to the customer's complaint without interrupting or becoming defensive. Acknowledge their frustration and let them know you're there to help.
- **Empathize:** Show empathy for the customer's situation and let them know you understand

their frustration. Avoid making excuses or blaming others.
- **Apologize:** Apologize for the inconvenience caused, even if the issue wasn't directly your fault. A sincere apology can go a long way in diffusing a tense situation.
- **Offer Solutions:** Work with the customer to find a solution that addresses their concerns. This could involve offering a refund, a discount, or a free wash.
- **Follow Up:** After resolving the issue, follow up with the customer to ensure their satisfaction. This shows that you value their business and are committed to providing excellent service.
- **Learn from Mistakes:** Use customer complaints as an opportunity to identify areas where you can improve your services or procedures. Implement changes to prevent similar issues from happening again.
- **Train Your Staff:** Train your staff on how to handle customer complaints professionally and effectively. Empower them to resolve issues on the spot whenever possible.

By handling customer complaints promptly and professionally, you can turn a negative experience into a positive one, building customer loyalty and enhancing your reputation.

6.5 Ensuring a Safe and Secure Environment

Creating a safe and secure environment for your customers and staff is a top priority for any laundromat owner. This involves implementing various measures to prevent accidents, deter theft, and protect your business from liability.

Here are some tips for ensuring a safe and secure environment in your laundromat:

- **Security Cameras:** Install security cameras in strategic locations throughout your laundromat, including entrances, exits, laundry areas, folding tables, and parking lots. Use high-resolution cameras with night vision capabilities and ensure they are properly maintained.
- **Alarm Systems:** Install a reliable alarm system that includes door and window sensors, motion detectors, and a loud siren. Connect the alarm system to a central monitoring station for 24/7 surveillance.
- **Secure Entry and Exit:** Ensure that your laundromat has secure entry and exit points. Use sturdy locks on doors and windows, and consider installing a buzzer system for after-hours access.
- **Employee Training:** Train your staff on safety protocols, including how to respond to emergencies, handle conflicts, and identify suspicious activity. Ensure they are familiar with the location of fire extinguishers, first-aid kits, and emergency exits.
- **Clear Signage:** Post clear and visible signage throughout your laundromat to indicate

emergency exits, safety procedures, and instructions for using machines and chemicals.
- **Regular Inspections:** Conduct regular inspections of your premises to identify and address potential hazards. Check for loose wires, leaks, or other safety issues.
- **Insurance:** Obtain adequate insurance coverage for your laundromat to protect your business from liability in case of accidents or injuries.
- **Maintenance and Repairs:** Regularly maintain and repair your equipment to prevent malfunctions and accidents. Keep a log of all maintenance and repairs for future reference.
- **Customer Awareness:** Encourage customers to be vigilant about their belongings and report any suspicious activity to staff. Provide lockers or secure storage areas for customers to store their valuables.
- **Community Policing:** Build relationships with local law enforcement and community organizations to enhance security and deter crime. Participate in neighborhood watch programs or business improvement districts.

By taking these proactive measures, you can create a safe and secure environment for your customers and staff, minimizing the risk of accidents, theft, and other security incidents. A safe and secure laundromat not only protects your investment but also enhances your reputation and attracts more customers.

6.6 Utilizing Technology to Streamline Operations

In today's digital age, technology plays a crucial role in streamlining laundromat operations, enhancing efficiency, and improving the customer experience. From laundromat management software to mobile payment options and online booking systems, technology can revolutionize the way you run your business.

Here are some ways to leverage technology in your laundromat:

- **Laundromat Management Software:** Invest in laundromat management software to automate various tasks, such as scheduling, inventory management, customer tracking, and financial reporting. This software can save you time and money, allowing you to focus on other aspects of your business.
- **Mobile Payment Options:** Offer mobile payment options like Apple Pay or Google Pay to cater to tech-savvy customers. This can streamline the payment process and reduce the need for cash handling.
- **Online Booking Systems:** Implement an online booking system for wash-and-fold services. This allows customers to schedule pickups and deliveries at their convenience, enhancing their experience and streamlining your operations.
- **Smart Laundry Solutions:** Explore smart laundry solutions that allow customers to

monitor their laundry cycles remotely through a mobile app. This can reduce wait times and improve the overall customer experience.
- **Security Systems:** Integrate your security cameras and alarm systems with your laundromat management software for seamless monitoring and control. This can enhance security and provide you with real-time alerts in case of any incidents.
- **Customer Wi-Fi:** Offer free Wi-Fi to your customers. This can enhance their experience and encourage them to spend more time in your laundromat, potentially increasing revenue from vending machines or other services.
- **Digital Signage:** Utilize digital signage to display promotions, pricing information, laundry tips, or entertainment content. This can create a more engaging and informative environment for your customers.

By embracing technology, you can streamline your operations, improve efficiency, reduce costs, and enhance the customer experience. This can lead to increased customer satisfaction, loyalty, and ultimately, a more profitable business.

6.7 Staying Up-to-Date on Industry Trends

The laundromat industry is constantly evolving, with new technologies, trends, and regulations emerging regularly. Staying up-to-date on these developments is crucial for remaining competitive and adapting your business to meet changing customer needs.

Here are some ways to stay informed about industry trends:

- **Industry Publications:** Subscribe to industry publications like American Coin-Op, Planet Laundry, or Coin Laundry Association newsletters to stay abreast of the latest news, trends, and best practices in the laundromat industry.
- **Trade Shows and Conferences:** Attend industry trade shows and conferences to network with other laundromat owners, learn about new products and technologies, and gain insights into emerging trends.
- **Online Forums and Communities:** Join online forums and communities for laundromat owners to share ideas, ask questions, and learn from the experiences of others.
- **Social Media:** Follow industry influencers, suppliers, and other laundromats on social media to stay informed about new developments and trends.
- **Market Research:** Conduct regular market research to understand changing customer preferences, identify emerging trends, and assess the competitive landscape.

By staying informed about industry trends, you can anticipate changes, adapt your business strategies, and remain at the forefront of the laundromat industry. This can lead to increased innovation, improved efficiency, and a stronger competitive edge.

Chapter 7

Marketing and Growing Your Laundromat – Spinning Your Way to Success

Welcome back, laundry aficionados! Your laundromat is up and running, the machines are churning, and customers are starting to discover your laundry haven. But the journey doesn't stop at opening day. Now it's time to shift gears and focus on marketing and growing your business.

Marketing is the engine that drives customer acquisition, retention, and ultimately, profitability. It's about creating a strong brand identity, reaching your target audience, and communicating the unique value proposition of your laundromat. Growing your laundromat involves expanding your services, exploring new revenue streams, and building a loyal customer base that keeps coming back for more.

In this chapter, we'll delve into the exciting world of laundromat marketing and growth strategies. We'll cover everything from building a compelling brand identity to creating effective marketing campaigns, utilizing online and offline advertising, leveraging social media for engagement, offering special promotions and discounts, expanding your services, and forging strategic partnerships. By the end of this chapter, you'll be equipped with a toolbox of marketing and growth strategies to elevate your laundromat to new heights.

So, let's put on our marketing hats, unleash our creativity, and embark on this exciting journey to make your laundromat a household name in your community.

7.1 Building a Strong Brand Identity

Your brand is more than just a logo or a name; it's the essence of your laundromat, the personality that sets you apart from the competition. A strong brand identity creates a lasting impression on your customers, fosters loyalty, and helps you stand out in a crowded market.

Here's how to build a strong brand identity for your laundromat:

- **Define Your Values:** What are the core values that drive your business? Are you committed to sustainability, customer service, innovation, or community engagement? Your brand identity should reflect these values and resonate with your target audience.
- **Develop a Brand Story:** Craft a compelling brand story that communicates your laundromat's history, mission, and unique value proposition. What inspired you to start this business? What challenges have you overcome? What makes your laundromat special? Your brand story should be authentic,

relatable, and inspire an emotional connection with your customers.
- **Visual Identity:** Create a visually appealing logo, color palette, and typography that reflects your brand's personality and resonates with your target audience. Your visual identity should be consistent across all marketing materials, from your website and social media profiles to your in-store signage and promotional materials.
- **Tagline or Slogan:** Develop a catchy tagline or slogan that captures the essence of your brand and sticks in customers' minds. For example, "The cleanest clean in town" or "Your laundry's happy place."
- **Voice and Tone:** Establish a consistent voice and tone for your brand communications. This could be friendly, informative, humorous, or sophisticated, depending on your target audience and brand personality.
- **Brand Experience:** Ensure that your brand identity is reflected in every aspect of your laundromat experience, from the decor and ambiance to the customer service and cleanliness. Your brand should be a cohesive and consistent experience for your customers.

Building a strong brand identity takes time and effort, but it's an investment that will pay off in the long run. A well-defined brand can differentiate you from the competition, attract loyal customers, and drive long-term growth for your laundromat.

7.2 Creating Effective Marketing Campaigns

Marketing campaigns are strategic initiatives designed to promote your laundromat and attract new customers. A successful marketing campaign combines creativity, targeted messaging, and effective distribution channels to reach your desired audience and generate a positive response.

Here's how to create effective marketing campaigns for your laundromat:

1. **Set Clear Goals:** What do you want to achieve with your marketing campaign? Are you looking to increase brand awareness, attract new customers, promote a new service, or boost sales during a slow period? Clearly defining your goals will help you tailor your campaign and measure its success.
2. **Identify Your Target Audience:** Who are you trying to reach with your campaign? What are their needs, preferences, and pain points? Tailor your messaging and choose marketing channels that resonate with your target audience.
3. **Craft Compelling Messaging:** Develop clear, concise, and engaging messaging that highlights the benefits of your laundromat and addresses the needs of your target audience. Use persuasive language, strong visuals, and a call to action to motivate customers to take action.
4. **Choose the Right Channels:** Select marketing channels that are most likely to reach your

target audience. This could include online advertising, social media, local print publications, community events, direct mail, or partnerships with local businesses.
5. **Track and Measure:** Implement tracking mechanisms to measure the effectiveness of your campaign. Track website traffic, social media engagement, customer inquiries, and any promotional codes or discounts you offer. This data will help you assess the success of your campaign and make adjustments as needed.
6. **Budget and Resources:** Allocate a realistic budget for your marketing campaign, considering the cost of advertising, printing materials, promotional items, and any paid partnerships or sponsorships. Ensure you have the necessary resources to execute your campaign effectively.
7. **Creativity:** Don't be afraid to get creative with your marketing campaigns. Think outside the box and come up with unique ideas that will capture attention and leave a lasting impression on your target audience.

Here are some examples of effective marketing campaigns for laundromats:

- **New Customer Special:** Offer a discount or free wash to new customers to entice them to try your laundromat.
- **Loyalty Program:** Reward loyal customers with discounts, free washes, or exclusive perks.

- **Referral Program:** Encourage customers to refer their friends and family by offering rewards for successful referrals.
- **Themed Events:** Host themed events, such as a "Laundry Luau" or "Clean Clothes Carnival," to create a fun and engaging experience for customers.
- **Community Partnerships:** Partner with local businesses or organizations to cross-promote your services and reach a wider audience.
- **Contests and Giveaways:** Run contests or giveaways on social media or in-store to generate excitement and engagement.

By creating effective marketing campaigns, you can attract new customers, retain existing ones, and build a strong brand presence in your community.

7.3 Utilizing Online and Offline Advertising

In the digital age, online advertising has become a powerful tool for reaching a vast audience and promoting your laundromat. However, offline advertising still plays a crucial role in reaching local customers and building brand awareness in your community.

Here's how to utilize both online and offline advertising effectively for your laundromat:

Online Advertising:

- **Search Engine Advertising (SEA):** Run paid ads on search engines like Google or Bing to target users searching for specific keywords related to laundry services in your area. These ads can appear at the top of search results, increasing your visibility and driving traffic to your website.

- **Social Media Advertising:** Target specific demographics and interests on platforms like Facebook, Instagram, or Twitter to reach potential customers who are most likely to be interested in your services. You can use various ad formats, such as image ads, video ads, or carousel ads, to showcase your laundromat and its offerings.
- **Display Advertising:** Place banner ads on relevant websites or blogs that your target audience frequents. This can help you increase brand awareness and drive traffic to your website.
- **Remarketing:** Target users who have previously visited your website or interacted with your brand online with personalized ads that remind them of your laundromat and encourage them to return.
- **Influencer Marketing:** Partner with local influencers or bloggers who have a strong following in your community to promote your laundromat. They can create sponsored content, share reviews, or host giveaways to generate buzz and attract new customers.

Offline Advertising:

- **Print Advertising:** Place ads in local newspapers, magazines, or community newsletters. This can be an effective way to

reach older demographics or those who prefer traditional media.
- **Direct Mail:** Send targeted mailers to residents or businesses in your area. Include coupons, discounts, or information about your services to incentivize them to visit your laundromat.
- **Flyers and Brochures:** Distribute flyers or brochures in high-traffic areas, such as community centers, grocery stores, or apartment complexes. Place them on car windshields or in mailboxes to reach a wider audience.
- **Billboards and Signage:** If your budget allows, consider placing billboards or signage in strategic locations to increase brand visibility and attract passersby.
- **Community Events:** Participate in local events, such as fairs, festivals, or farmers markets, to promote your laundromat and connect with potential customers. Offer special discounts or giveaways to incentivize them to visit your laundromat.

By utilizing a combination of online and offline advertising, you can reach a broader audience, increase brand awareness, and drive more customers to your laundromat. Experiment with different channels and tactics to find what works best for your business and budget.

7.4 Leveraging Social Media for Engagement

Social media platforms offer a powerful way to connect with your customers, build relationships, and foster a sense of community around your laundromat brand. By leveraging social media strategically, you can increase brand awareness, drive traffic to your website, and encourage repeat business. Here are some tips for leveraging social media for laundromat engagement:

- **Post Regularly:** Share engaging content regularly on your social media channels. This could include photos of your clean and inviting space, customer testimonials, laundry tips and tricks, behind-the-scenes glimpses, and promotions or special offers.
- **Run Contests and Giveaways:** Engage your audience by running contests or giveaways that encourage them to like, share, or comment on your posts. This can help increase your reach and attract new followers.
- **Respond to Comments and Messages:** Engage with your audience by promptly responding to comments and messages. This shows that you value their feedback and are committed to providing excellent customer service.
- **Use Relevant Hashtags:** Use relevant hashtags to make your content discoverable by a wider audience. Some popular hashtags for laundromats include #laundryday, #cleanclothes, #washandfold, #laundromatlife, and #laundrylove.

- **Live Videos:** Go live on Facebook or Instagram to give your audience a virtual tour of your laundromat, showcase new equipment, or answer customer questions in real-time.
- **Stories and Reels:** Utilize the Stories or Reels feature on Instagram to share short, engaging videos that highlight your laundromat's unique features and personality.
- **Social Media Advertising:** Invest in targeted social media advertising to reach specific demographics or interests in your area. This can be an effective way to attract new customers and promote specific services or promotions.
- **Collaborate with Influencers:** Partner with local influencers or bloggers who have a following in your community to promote your laundromat. They can create sponsored content, share reviews, or offer exclusive discounts to their followers.
- **Community Building:** Create a Facebook group or online community for your customers to connect, share laundry tips, and ask questions. This can foster a sense of belonging and loyalty among your customer base.

By actively engaging with your audience on social media, you can build relationships, foster loyalty, and turn your laundromat into a thriving online community.

7.5 Offering Special Promotions and Discounts

Everyone loves a good deal! Offering special promotions and discounts is a proven strategy for attracting new customers, incentivizing repeat business, and boosting sales during slow periods.

Here are some creative promotion and discount ideas for your laundromat:

- **New Customer Special:** Offer a discount or free wash to first-time customers to entice them to try your services.
- **Loyalty Rewards:** Reward frequent customers with discounts, free washes, or exclusive perks after a certain number of visits or spending a specific amount.
- **Referral Bonus:** Offer a discount or reward to customers who refer their friends and family to your laundromat.
- **Happy Hour:** Offer discounted rates during off-peak hours to incentivize customers to visit during less busy times.
- **Wash-and-Fold Bundle:** Offer a discounted package deal for customers who use both wash-and-fold and dry cleaning services.
- **Bulk Discounts:** Offer discounts for customers who bring in large loads of laundry or purchase multiple laundry bags.
- **Holiday Promotions:** Run special promotions during holidays or seasonal events, such as a "Spring Cleaning Special" or a "Back-to-School Discount."
- **Themed Events:** Host themed events, such as a "Laundry Luau" or "Clean Clothes Carnival," and offer discounts or giveaways to participants.

- **Partner Promotions:** Partner with local businesses to offer cross-promotions or discounts. For example, you could partner with a nearby coffee shop to offer a discount on coffee to your laundromat customers.
- **Flash Sales:** Announce surprise flash sales on social media or through email to create a sense of urgency and excitement.

When offering promotions and discounts, be strategic about your pricing and ensure that you're still covering your costs and generating a profit. Track the success of your promotions to see what resonates with your customers and adjust your strategy as needed.

7.6 Expanding Your Services

As your laundromat gains traction, consider expanding your services to attract a wider customer base and increase revenue streams. Offering additional services can differentiate your laundromat from the competition and make it a one-stop shop for all laundry needs.

Here are some potential service expansions for your laundromat:

- **Wash-and-Fold:** This convenient service allows customers to drop off their laundry to be washed, dried, and folded by your staff. It's particularly popular among busy professionals and families who lack the time or desire to do laundry themselves.
- **Dry Cleaning:** Partner with a local dry cleaner or invest in your own dry-cleaning equipment

to offer this premium service. Dry cleaning caters to customers with delicate or specialty garments that require special care.
- **Ironing and Pressing:** Offer ironing and pressing services for customers who want their clothes to look crisp and professional.
- **Alterations and Repairs:** Partner with a seamstress or tailor to offer alteration and repair services. This can be a valuable addition for customers who need minor adjustments to their clothing.
- **Shoe Repair:** Partner with a shoe repair specialist to offer shoe cleaning, polishing, and repair services. This can attract customers who need their shoes fixed or maintained.
- **Vending Machines:** Expand your vending machine offerings beyond snacks and drinks. Consider adding laundry supplies, such as detergent, fabric softener, and dryer sheets. You could also offer other essentials like phone chargers, headphones, or travel-sized toiletries.
- **Pickup and Delivery:** Offer pickup and delivery services for added convenience, especially for customers who are elderly, disabled, or simply too busy to visit your laundromat.
- **Commercial Laundry:** Cater to local businesses by offering commercial laundry services for items like uniforms, linens, or towels. This can be a lucrative revenue stream, especially if you're located near hotels, restaurants, or healthcare facilities.

- **Specialty Services:** Consider offering niche services like pet-friendly washing, eco-friendly laundry, or even a laundromat café where customers can enjoy coffee and snacks while they wait.

By expanding your services, you can cater to a wider range of customer needs and increase your revenue potential. Be sure to market your new services effectively and train your staff to deliver them with the same level of quality and care as your core laundromat services.

7.7 Building Strategic Partnerships

Building strategic partnerships with other businesses or organizations in your community can be a powerful way to expand your reach, attract new customers, and enhance your brand reputation.

Here are some potential partnerships for your laundromat:

- **Local Businesses:** Partner with local businesses like dry cleaners, tailors, shoe repair shops, or even coffee shops to offer cross-promotions or discounts to each other's customers.
- **Apartment Complexes and Student Housing:** Offer discounts or special deals to residents of nearby apartment complexes or student housing facilities. Consider setting up a referral program where property managers recommend your laundromat to their tenants.

- **Community Organizations:** Partner with local charities or non-profit organizations to host fundraising events or donate a portion of your proceeds to their cause. This can generate positive publicity and goodwill in your community.
- **Schools and Universities:** Partner with local schools or universities to offer laundry services for sports teams, dorms, or other student groups.
- **Hotels and Hospitality:** Offer commercial laundry services to local hotels, motels, or bed and breakfasts. This can provide a steady stream of revenue and build lasting relationships with local businesses.
- **Local Government:** Explore opportunities to partner with your local government to provide laundry services for community centers, shelters, or other public facilities.

By building strategic partnerships, you can tap into new customer bases, expand your service offerings, and strengthen your presence in the community.

Chapter 8

Managing Finances and Maximizing Profit – The Art of Laundry Economics

Welcome back, aspiring laundry tycoons! Now that your laundromat is operational, it's time to delve into the financial intricacies of running a successful business. This is where the numbers come to life, where revenue streams meet expenses, and where strategic decisions pave the path to profitability.

Managing finances and maximizing profit are essential skills for any business owner, and laundromats are no exception. In this chapter, we'll unravel the secrets of laundromat economics, providing you with a comprehensive understanding of financial statements, revenue and expense tracking, pricing strategies, budgeting for growth, cash flow management, accounting software, and tax and legal considerations.

So, grab your calculators and spreadsheets, put on your financial analyst hats, and let's explore the fascinating world of laundry finance.

8.1 Understanding Laundromat Financial Statements

Financial statements are the backbone of any business, providing a snapshot of its financial health and performance. For laundromat owners, understanding these statements is crucial for making informed decisions, tracking progress, and ensuring long-term profitability.

Here are the three key financial statements you need to understand:

1. **Income Statement (Profit and Loss Statement):** This statement summarizes your laundromat's revenues and expenses over a specific period, usually a month, quarter, or year. It shows your net income (profit) or net loss, which is the difference between your total revenue and total expenses.
2. **Balance Sheet:** This statement provides a snapshot of your laundromat's financial position at a specific point in time. It lists your assets (what you own), liabilities (what you owe), and equity (the difference between your assets and liabilities).
3. **Cash Flow Statement:** This statement tracks the flow of cash in and out of your business. It shows how much cash you generated from operations, how much you invested, and how much you borrowed or repaid.

By analyzing these financial statements, you can gain valuable insights into your laundromat's financial health, identify trends, and make informed decisions about pricing, expenses, and investments. For example, if your income statement shows a decline in revenue, you can investigate the reasons behind it and adjust your marketing or pricing strategies accordingly. If your balance sheet shows a high level of debt, you may need to focus on reducing expenses or increasing revenue to improve your financial stability.

8.2 Tracking Revenue and Expenses

Tracking your laundromat's revenue and expenses is essential for understanding your cash flow, identifying areas for improvement, and making informed financial decisions. It allows you to monitor your profitability, track your progress toward financial goals, and detect any potential issues early on.

Here's how to effectively track your revenue and expenses:

- **Categorize Transactions:** Categorize all your transactions into specific categories, such as revenue from self-service machines, wash-and-fold services, vending machines, and other sources. For expenses, categorize them into categories like rent, utilities, payroll, supplies, maintenance, and marketing.
- **Use Accounting Software:** Invest in accounting software to automate the tracking process and generate accurate financial reports. Popular options include QuickBooks, Xero, and FreshBooks. These software programs can streamline your bookkeeping, simplify tax preparation, and provide valuable insights into your financial performance.

- **Reconcile Accounts:** Regularly reconcile your bank and credit card statements with your accounting records to ensure accuracy and identify any discrepancies.
- **Monitor Key Metrics:** Track key metrics like revenue per machine, average transaction value, and expense ratios. This will help you assess your laundromat's efficiency and identify areas for improvement.
- **Analyze Trends:** Analyze your revenue and expense trends over time to identify patterns, seasonality, and potential areas for growth or cost reduction.

By diligently tracking and analyzing your financial data, you can gain a deeper understanding of your laundromat's financial performance and make informed decisions to optimize profitability.

8.3 Implementing Pricing Strategies

Setting the right prices for your laundromat services is a delicate balancing act. Your prices need to be competitive to attract customers, but they also need to cover your costs and generate a profit. Implementing effective pricing strategies can help you achieve this balance and maximize your revenue potential.

Here are some pricing strategies for laundromats:

1. **Cost-Plus Pricing:** This strategy involves calculating your total costs per wash (including water, electricity, detergent, labor, and overhead) and then adding a markup to

determine your price. This ensures that your prices cover your costs and generate a profit.
2. **Competitive Pricing:** Research the prices charged by other laundromats in your area and set your prices accordingly. You can differentiate yourself by offering additional services or amenities, but your base prices should be competitive.
3. **Value-Based Pricing:** If your laundromat offers premium services or amenities, such as wash-and-fold, dry cleaning, or a comfortable lounge area, consider value-based pricing. This involves charging a higher price based on the perceived value and convenience you offer.
4. **Tiered Pricing:** Offer different prices for different machine sizes or wash cycles. This allows customers to choose the option that best suits their needs and budget.
5. **Time-of-Day Pricing:** Charge lower prices during off-peak hours to incentivize customers to visit during less busy times. This can help to distribute demand more evenly throughout the day and avoid overcrowding during peak hours.
6. **Bundled Pricing:** Offer discounts or package deals for customers who use multiple services, such as wash-and-fold and dry cleaning. This can encourage customers to try new services and increase your average transaction value.
7. **Dynamic Pricing:** Consider using dynamic pricing, where prices fluctuate based on demand, time of day, or other factors. This can help you maximize revenue during peak hours

and attract customers during slower periods with lower prices.

Remember, pricing is not a one-time decision. Regularly review and adjust your pricing strategy to reflect changes in your costs, competition, and customer demand.

8.4 Budgeting for Growth and Expansion

As your laundromat starts to generate a steady income, it's essential to start thinking about growth and expansion. This could involve opening additional locations, adding new services, upgrading your equipment, or expanding your marketing efforts.

Here are some tips for budgeting for growth and expansion:

- **Set Financial Goals:** Define your growth goals and create a financial plan to achieve them. This could include targets for revenue growth, profit margins, or new customer acquisition.
- **Create a Budget:** Develop a detailed budget that outlines the costs associated with your growth plans. This could include expenses for new equipment, marketing campaigns, staff training, or leasehold improvements.
- **Secure Funding:** If you need additional capital to finance your growth, explore various funding options like small business loans, equipment financing, or crowdfunding.
- **Prioritize Investments:** Identify the most critical investments for your growth strategy

and prioritize them based on their potential return on investment (ROI).
- **Track Your Progress:** Regularly track your progress towards your growth goals and adjust your budget and strategies as needed.

By planning and budgeting for growth, you can ensure that your laundromat is prepared to take advantage of new opportunities and expand its reach in the market.

8.5 Managing Cash Flow Effectively

Cash flow is the lifeblood of any business. It refers to the movement of cash in and out of your laundromat. Positive cash flow means you have more money coming in than going out, while negative cash flow means the opposite.

Effective cash flow management is crucial for ensuring that you have enough money to cover your expenses, pay your bills on time, and invest in growth opportunities.

Here are some tips for managing your laundromat's cash flow:

- **Forecast Cash Flow:** Create a cash flow forecast to project your future cash inflows and outflows. This will help you identify potential cash flow shortages and take corrective action before they become a problem.
- **Invoice Promptly:** Invoice your customers promptly for wash-and-fold services or any

other services you offer. Follow up on unpaid invoices promptly.
- **Offer Multiple Payment Options:** Accept cash, credit cards, debit cards, and mobile payments to provide convenience for your customers and ensure a steady flow of cash.
- **Negotiate Payment Terms:** Negotiate favorable payment terms with your suppliers, such as extended payment periods or early payment discounts.
- **Control Expenses:** Monitor your expenses closely and look for ways to cut costs without sacrificing quality or service.
- **Maintain a Cash Reserve:** Set aside a portion of your profits in a cash reserve to cover unexpected expenses or downturns in business.

By managing your cash flow effectively, you can ensure that your laundromat has the financial resources it needs to operate smoothly, invest in growth, and weather any financial storms.

8.6 Utilizing Accounting Software

Accounting software can be a valuable tool for laundromat owners, streamlining financial management, improving accuracy, and providing valuable insights into your business's financial performance.

Here are some benefits of using accounting software for your laundromat:

- **Automation:** Accounting software automates many tedious and time-consuming tasks, such as data entry, invoice generation, and bank reconciliations. This frees up your time to focus on other aspects of your business.
- **Accuracy:** Accounting software helps reduce errors and ensure accurate financial records. This is essential for tax preparation and making informed financial decisions.

Reporting: Accounting software generates comprehensive financial reports, such as income statements, balance sheets, and cash flow statements. This gives you a comprehensive view of your financial performance and helps you identify areas for improvement.

- **Tax Preparation:** Accounting software simplifies tax preparation by automatically calculating taxes and generating the necessary reports for filing. This can save you time and money, as well as reduce the risk of errors.
- **Financial Analysis:** Many accounting software programs offer financial analysis tools that can help you track key metrics, identify trends, and forecast future performance. This can guide your decision-making and help you optimize your financial strategies.
- **Cloud-Based Access:** Cloud-based accounting software allows you to access your financial data from anywhere, anytime, using any internet-connected device. This provides

flexibility and convenience for managing your finances on the go.

When choosing accounting software for your laundromat, consider factors like ease of use, features, pricing, and customer support. Some popular options for small businesses include:

- QuickBooks Online: A user-friendly cloud-based accounting software with a wide range of features, including invoicing, expense tracking, and reporting.
- Xero: A cloud-based accounting software designed for small businesses, offering features like invoicing, bank reconciliation, and payroll integration.
- FreshBooks: A cloud-based accounting software that simplifies invoicing and expense tracking, making it ideal for service-based businesses like laundromats.
- Wave: A free cloud-based accounting software that offers basic features like invoicing, expense tracking, and financial reporting.

By utilizing accounting software, you can streamline your financial management, improve accuracy, and gain valuable insights into your laundromat's financial performance.

8.7 Minimizing Taxes and Legal Liabilities

As a laundromat owner, it's essential to be aware of your tax obligations and take steps to minimize your tax burden legally. Additionally, understanding and adhering to legal requirements can help you avoid costly fines and penalties.

Here are some tips for minimizing taxes and legal liabilities:

1. **Tax Deductions:** Take advantage of all eligible tax deductions for your laundromat business. This could include deductions for rent, utilities, supplies, repairs, depreciation, and advertising expenses. Consult with a tax professional to ensure you're claiming all eligible deductions.
2. **Tax Credits:** Research tax credits available for small businesses, such as the Small Business Health Care Tax Credit or the Work Opportunity Tax Credit. These credits can significantly reduce your tax liability.
3. **Business Structure:** Choose a business structure that offers tax advantages, such as an S corporation or a limited liability company (LLC). These structures can help you minimize self-employment taxes and protect your personal assets from business liabilities.
4. **Legal Compliance:** Ensure that your laundromat complies with all local, state, and federal regulations. This includes obtaining necessary permits and licenses, adhering to safety and health standards, and complying with environmental regulations.
5. **Insurance:** Obtain adequate insurance coverage to protect your business from liability in case of accidents, injuries, or property damage.
6. **Record Keeping:** Maintain accurate and organized financial records to substantiate your tax deductions and ensure compliance with tax laws.

7. **Professional Advice:** Consult with a tax professional or attorney to ensure you're following all tax laws and regulations and taking advantage of all available deductions and credits.

By proactively managing your taxes and legal obligations, you can minimize your financial burden, protect your business from liabilities, and ensure the long-term sustainability of your laundromat.

Chapter 9

Ensuring Legal Compliance – Navigating the Legal Landscape of Laundromat Ownership

Welcome back, aspiring laundry moguls! In this chapter, we'll delve into the legal aspects of running a laundromat. While not as exciting as picking out the perfect shade of blue for your washing machines or crafting witty social media posts, understanding and adhering to legal requirements is crucial for protecting your business, ensuring its longevity, and avoiding costly fines or penalties.

Consider this chapter your legal compass, guiding you through the complex terrain of licenses, permits, regulations, intellectual property, insurance, employee matters, and taxes. We'll unravel the legalese, demystify the jargon, and provide you with practical advice to ensure your laundromat operates within the boundaries of the law.

So, grab your legal pads and magnifying glasses as we embark on this journey to ensure your laundry business is legally compliant and protected.

9.1 Obtaining Necessary Business Licenses and Permits

Before you can legally open your laundromat's doors, you'll need to obtain a variety of licenses and permits. These legal documents ensure that your business complies with local, state, and federal regulations and operates in a safe and ethical manner.

The specific licenses and permits required vary depending on your location and the nature of your business. However, some common ones include:

1. **Business License:** This is the most basic license required to operate any business, including a laundromat. It registers your business with the government and allows you to legally conduct business activities. The application process and fees vary depending on your location.
2. **Sales Tax Permit:** If you plan to sell laundry products like detergent, fabric softener, or dryer sheets, or if you offer wash-and-fold services, you'll likely need a sales tax permit. This allows you to collect sales tax from customers and remit it to the government.
3. **Employer Identification Number (EIN):** An EIN is a unique nine-digit number assigned by the IRS to identify your business for tax purposes. You'll need an EIN if you have employees or if you operate your laundromat as a corporation or partnership.

4. **Federal Tax ID Number:** This is similar to an EIN and is required for businesses that sell goods or services subject to federal excise tax, such as laundry services.
5. **Health Permit:** Laundromats are subject to health inspections to ensure they meet sanitation and hygiene standards. Obtaining a health permit involves passing inspections of your facility and equipment to ensure they comply with health codes.
6. **Fire Safety Permit:** To ensure the safety of your customers and staff, you'll need a fire safety permit. This involves passing inspections of your fire suppression systems, emergency exits, and fire safety equipment.
7. **Environmental Permit:** Depending on your location and the type of equipment you use, you may need an environmental permit to address wastewater disposal and other environmental concerns. This is especially important if your laundromat uses large amounts of water or discharges wastewater into the municipal system.
8. **Sign Permit:** If you plan to display signage for your laundromat, you'll need a sign permit. This ensures that your signs comply with local regulations regarding size, placement, and content.
9. **Building Permit:** If you plan to construct or renovate a building for your laundromat, you'll need a building permit. This ensures that the construction complies with local building codes and safety standards.

The process for obtaining licenses and permits can be time-consuming and complex. It's essential to start the process early and consult with local government agencies or business development centers to ensure you have all the necessary documentation and meet all requirements.

9.2 Complying with Local and Federal Regulations

In addition to obtaining the necessary licenses and permits, laundromat owners must also comply with a variety of local, state, and federal regulations. These regulations cover aspects like safety, health, environmental protection, consumer protection, and employment laws.

Here's a breakdown of some key regulations you need to be aware of:

- **Safety Regulations:** Laundromats must comply with safety regulations to ensure the well-being of customers and staff. This includes maintaining safe equipment, providing adequate ventilation, ensuring proper fire safety measures, and having a plan for handling emergencies.
- **Health Regulations:** Health regulations are in place to ensure that laundromats maintain a clean and hygienic environment. This includes regular cleaning and disinfection of machines, floors, restrooms, and common areas. Laundromats must also comply with

regulations regarding wastewater disposal and the handling of chemicals.
- **Environmental Regulations:** Laundromats are required to comply with environmental regulations to minimize their impact on the environment. This may involve using energy-efficient equipment, recycling water, and properly disposing of hazardous waste.
- **Consumer Protection Regulations:** Consumer protection regulations are designed to protect customers from unfair or deceptive business practices. Laundromats must comply with regulations regarding pricing, advertising, and refund policies.
- **Employment Laws:** If you have employees, you must comply with employment laws, including minimum wage laws, overtime regulations, anti-discrimination laws, and workplace safety regulations.

Staying informed about and complying with all applicable regulations is crucial for the success of your laundromat. Non-compliance can result in fines, penalties, and even closure of your business. It's essential to stay up-to-date on any changes in regulations and consult with legal professionals if you have any questions or concerns.

9.3 Protecting Your Intellectual Property

Intellectual property (IP) refers to creations of the mind, such as inventions, literary and artistic works, designs, and symbols, names, and images used in commerce. Protecting your intellectual property is essential for safeguarding your brand identity, preventing others from copying your ideas, and ensuring that you reap the benefits of your creativity and innovation.

Here are some types of intellectual property that you may need to protect in your laundromat business:

- **Trademark:** A trademark is a word, phrase, symbol, or design that identifies and distinguishes the source of goods or services. You can trademark your laundromat's name, logo, or slogan to prevent others from using them without your permission.
- **Copyright:** Copyright protects original works of authorship, such as literary, dramatic, musical, and artistic works. You can copyright any original marketing materials, website content, or other creative works you create for your laundromat.
- **Trade Secret:** A trade secret is confidential business information that gives you a competitive advantage. This could include your secret cleaning formula, your customer list, or your marketing strategies. You can protect trade secrets by keeping them confidential and using non-disclosure agreements with employees and contractors.
- **Patent:** A patent grants you the exclusive right to make, use, or sell an invention for a limited period of time. If you develop a new type of washing machine or a unique laundry process,

you could potentially patent it to prevent others from copying your invention.

To protect your intellectual property, consider registering your trademarks and copyrights with the appropriate government agencies. Use non-disclosure agreements to protect trade secrets, and consult with an intellectual property attorney if you have any questions or concerns about protecting your IP.

9.4 Understanding Insurance Requirements

Insurance is essential for protecting your laundromat from financial losses due to unexpected events like accidents, injuries, property damage, or lawsuits. Having the right insurance coverage can provide peace of mind and ensure the continuity of your business in the face of adversity.

Here are some types of insurance you should consider for your laundromat:

- **General Liability Insurance:** This covers bodily injury and property damage claims made by third parties. For example, if a customer slips and falls in your laundromat, general liability insurance can cover their medical expenses and legal fees.
- **Property Insurance:** This covers damage to your laundromat's building and its contents, such as equipment, furniture, and inventory, due to fire, theft, vandalism, or natural disasters.

- **Business Interruption Insurance:** This covers lost income and ongoing expenses if your laundromat is forced to close temporarily due to a covered event, such as a fire or flood.
- **Workers' Compensation Insurance:** If you have employees, you're legally required to have workers' compensation insurance. This covers medical expenses and lost wages for employees who are injured or become ill on the job.
- **Cyber Liability Insurance:** This covers losses due to cyberattacks, such as data breaches, ransomware attacks, or business interruption.
- **Employment Practices Liability Insurance (EPLI):** This covers claims related to employment practices, such as discrimination, harassment, or wrongful termination.

When choosing insurance for your laundromat, consider the specific risks associated with your business and the level of coverage you need. Consult with an insurance agent who specializes in commercial insurance to help you choose the right policies for your needs.

9.5 Handling Employee Matters (If Applicable)

If you have employees in your laundromat, you'll need to navigate various legal and administrative matters related to employment. This includes compliance with employment laws, payroll processing, record keeping, and employee relations.

Here are some key aspects of handling employee matters:

- **Employment Contracts:** Have written employment contracts in place for all employees. The contracts should clearly outline the terms of employment, including job duties, compensation, benefits, and termination policies.
- **Payroll and Taxes:** Set up a payroll system to process employee wages and withholdings accurately. Comply with federal and state payroll tax regulations and file the necessary tax forms on time.

Employee Handbook: Create an employee handbook that outlines your company's policies and procedures regarding dress code, attendance, breaks, safety, and conduct. Make sure the handbook is clear, comprehensive, and up-to-date with relevant labor laws.

- **Timekeeping and Attendance:** Implement a reliable timekeeping system to track employee hours accurately. Establish clear policies for clocking in and out, requesting time off, and reporting absences.
- **Performance Reviews:** Conduct regular performance reviews to provide feedback to employees on their strengths and areas for improvement. Use performance reviews to set goals, discuss career development

opportunities, and address any performance issues.
- **Conflict Resolution:** Establish a formal process for handling employee complaints or conflicts. Ensure that employees feel comfortable raising concerns without fear of retaliation and that their concerns are addressed promptly and fairly.
- **Termination:** Develop clear termination policies and procedures that comply with labor laws. Provide written notice of termination, conduct exit interviews, and ensure proper documentation is maintained.

By proactively managing employee matters, you can create a positive and productive work environment where employees feel valued, motivated, and supported. This can lead to increased employee satisfaction, loyalty, and ultimately, improved customer service and business performance.

9.6 Navigating Tax Obligations

As a laundromat owner, you're responsible for various tax obligations at the federal, state, and local levels. Understanding and complying with these obligations is crucial for avoiding penalties and maintaining the financial health of your business.

Here are some key tax obligations for laundromat owners:

- **Income Tax:** Laundromats are required to pay federal and state income tax on their profits. The tax rate varies depending on your business structure and income level. Consult with a tax professional to determine your specific tax obligations and take advantage of any available deductions or credits.

- **Sales Tax:** If you sell laundry products or offer wash-and-fold services, you'll likely need to collect and remit sales tax to the state. The sales tax rate varies depending on your location and the type of goods or services you offer.
- **Payroll Tax:** If you have employees, you're responsible for withholding payroll taxes from their wages and paying employer payroll taxes. This includes Social Security and Medicare taxes, federal unemployment tax, and state unemployment tax.
- **Property Tax:** If you own the building where your laundromat is located, you'll need to pay property tax. The tax rate varies depending on the value of your property and the local tax rates.
- **Self-Employment Tax:** If you're a sole proprietor or a partner in a partnership, you'll need to pay self-employment tax, which covers Social Security and Medicare taxes.
- **Excise Tax:** Some states impose an excise tax on laundry services. This tax is typically a percentage of the gross receipts from laundry services.

To navigate your tax obligations effectively, consider hiring a qualified accountant or tax professional. They can help you understand your specific tax requirements, prepare and file your tax returns, and ensure you're taking advantage of all available deductions and credits.

9.7 Staying Informed on Legal Changes

Laws and regulations are constantly evolving, and it's essential for laundromat owners to stay informed about any changes that may affect their business. Failing to comply with new regulations can result in fines, penalties, or even the closure of your business.

Here are some ways to stay informed about legal changes:

- **Industry Associations:** Join industry associations like the Coin Laundry Association (CLA) or your state's laundromat association. These organizations provide valuable resources, including updates on legal changes, industry news, and best practices.
- **Legal Counsel:** Consult with an attorney who specializes in business law to stay informed about legal developments that may affect your laundromat. They can also help you review contracts, address legal issues, and ensure compliance with regulations.
- **Government Websites:** Regularly check the websites of relevant government agencies, such as the Small Business Administration (SBA), the Department of Labor (DOL), and the Environmental Protection Agency (EPA), for

updates on regulations and compliance requirements.
- **Newsletters and Alerts:** Subscribe to newsletters or alerts from government agencies or industry associations to receive timely updates on legal changes.
- **Continuing Education:** Participate in continuing education courses or webinars on legal topics relevant to your business. This can help you stay abreast of new developments and ensure you're operating your laundromat in a legally compliant manner.

By staying informed and proactive, you can adapt your business practices to comply with new regulations, avoid legal issues, and ensure the long-term success of your laundromat.

Chapter 10

Technology and Innovation in Laundromats – The Digital Transformation of Laundry Day

Welcome back, laundry pioneers! In this chapter, we're venturing into the exciting realm of technology and innovation, where the laundromat experience is being transformed by cutting-edge solutions. We're not just talking about faster spin cycles or bigger dryers – we're talking about a complete digital makeover that's revolutionizing the way we do laundry.

Gone are the days of fumbling for quarters and waiting anxiously for machines to finish. Today's laundromats are embracing technology to create a seamless, convenient, and even enjoyable experience for customers. From mobile payment apps and smart laundry solutions to online booking systems and eco-friendly practices, technology is redefining what it means to run a successful laundromat in the 21st century.

In this chapter, we'll delve into the latest technological advancements and innovative practices that are shaping the future of the laundromat industry. We'll explore how you can leverage these tools to enhance customer satisfaction, streamline operations, boost profitability, and gain a competitive edge in the market. So, fasten your seatbelts and prepare for a thrilling ride into the digital transformation of laundry day.

10.1 Leveraging Laundromat Management Software

Laundromat management software is the digital backbone of modern laundry businesses. It's a comprehensive suite of tools designed to streamline operations, improve efficiency, and enhance the customer experience. Think of it as your digital assistant, managing everything from machine scheduling and payment processing to inventory tracking and customer relationship management.

Here are some key features and benefits of laundromat management software:

- **Machine Scheduling:** Customers can view machine availability in real-time, reserve machines in advance, and receive notifications when their laundry cycle is complete. This eliminates the need for customers to wait around for available machines, improving their experience and reducing congestion in your laundromat.
- **Cashless Payments:** Customers can pay for laundry services using their smartphones, credit cards, or digital wallets. This eliminates the need for cash handling, reduces the risk of theft, and provides a convenient payment option for customers.

- **Remote Monitoring and Control:** Laundromat owners can remotely monitor machine usage, track revenue, and control machine settings from their smartphones or computers. This allows for real-time troubleshooting, energy optimization, and enhanced security.
- **Customer Relationship Management (CRM):** Track customer data, such as usage frequency, spending habits, and preferences, to tailor your marketing efforts and loyalty programs. This personalized approach can help you build stronger relationships with your customers and increase loyalty.
- **Inventory Management:** Track inventory levels of laundry supplies like detergent, fabric softener, and dryer sheets. Automate reordering to ensure you never run out of essential items.
- **Reporting and Analytics:** Generate detailed reports on sales, revenue, expenses, and customer behavior. This data can help you identify trends, track your performance, and make informed business decisions.

Here are some popular laundromat management software options:

- **Washlava:** A comprehensive platform offering mobile payments, machine scheduling, remote monitoring, and marketing tools.
- **LaundryPulse:** Provides real-time machine monitoring, cashless payments, customer loyalty programs, and marketing automation.

- **Cents:** Offers a suite of tools for managing laundry operations, including mobile payments, machine scheduling, remote monitoring, and marketing solutions.
- **ShinePay:** A mobile payment platform specifically designed for laundromats, offering cashless payments, loyalty programs, and marketing features.
- **CleanCloud:** Provides a comprehensive solution for managing laundry businesses, including online booking, scheduling, payment processing, and marketing tools.

The right laundromat management software can revolutionize your business, saving you time, money, and resources while enhancing the customer experience. When choosing a software solution, consider your specific needs, budget, and the size of your laundromat.

10.2 Implementing Mobile Payment Options

In today's cashless society, mobile payment options have become increasingly popular. By offering mobile payments in your laundromat, you can cater to the preferences of tech-savvy customers, streamline transactions, and reduce the need for cash handling.

Here are some common mobile payment options for laundromats:

- **Apple Pay:** A mobile payment and digital wallet service by Apple Inc. that allows users to make payments using their iPhones or Apple Watches.

- **Google Pay:** A similar mobile payment service by Google that allows users to make payments using their Android phones or Wear OS smartwatches.
- **Samsung Pay:** A mobile payment service by Samsung Electronics that allows users to make payments using their Samsung smartphones.
- **Other Digital Wallets:** There are various other digital wallet options available, such as PayPal, Venmo, or Cash App.

To implement mobile payments in your laundromat, you'll need to partner with a payment processor that supports mobile transactions. Many laundromat management software platforms integrate with popular payment processors, making it easy to accept mobile payments.

Here's how mobile payments can benefit your laundromat:

- **Convenience:** Customers can pay for laundry services with a simple tap of their smartphone, eliminating the need to carry cash or coins.
- **Security:** Mobile payments are typically more secure than cash transactions, reducing the risk of theft or fraud.
- **Hygiene:** Mobile payments promote contactless transactions, which is especially important in the current health-conscious environment.
- **Customer Satisfaction:** Offering mobile payments caters to the preferences of tech-

savvy customers, enhancing their overall experience.
- **Increased Revenue:** Studies have shown that businesses that accept mobile payments tend to see an increase in sales, as customers are more likely to make impulse purchases when they don't have to fumble for cash.

By embracing mobile payment technology, you can modernize your laundromat and provide a convenient, secure, and hygienic payment option for your customers.

10.3 Utilizing Online Booking Systems

Online booking systems are revolutionizing the way customers access services, and laundromats are no exception. By implementing an online booking system for wash-and-fold services, you can offer your customers unparalleled convenience, streamline your operations, and increase efficiency.

Here's how online booking systems work for laundromats:

1. **Customer Interface:** Customers can access your online booking system through your website or a mobile app. They can select the type of service they need (wash-and-fold, dry cleaning, etc.), choose a pickup and delivery time, and make payment online.
2. **Order Management:** The booking system automatically generates an order for your staff,

including customer details, service requests, and payment information.
3. **Route Optimization:** If you offer pickup and delivery services, the booking system can optimize routes for your drivers, ensuring efficient and timely service.
4. **Communication:** The system can send automated notifications to customers, confirming their bookings, providing updates on their orders, and notifying them when their laundry is ready for pickup or delivery.

Here are some benefits of using an online booking system for your laundromat:

- **Convenience:** Customers can book services at their convenience, 24/7, without having to call or visit your laundromat in person.
- **Efficiency:** Automate the booking process, reducing manual tasks for your staff and minimizing errors.
- **Increased Revenue:** Online booking systems can attract new customers who prefer the convenience of booking online.
- **Customer Insights:** Gather valuable data on customer preferences, usage patterns, and peak booking times to optimize your operations and marketing efforts.
- **Improved Customer Experience:** Provide a seamless and convenient booking experience for your customers, enhancing their satisfaction and loyalty.

There are several online booking platforms available specifically for laundromats, such as LaundryHero, ScheduleOnce, and BookingKoala. These platforms offer features like customizable booking forms, automated reminders, payment processing, and integration with laundromat management software.

By implementing an online booking system, you can take your laundromat to the next level, offering customers a modern and convenient way to access your services while streamlining your operations and increasing efficiency.

10.4 Exploring Smart Laundry Solutions

Smart laundry solutions are revolutionizing the laundromat experience by leveraging technology to make laundry day easier, more convenient, and more efficient for customers. These solutions range from smart washers and dryers with advanced features to mobile apps that allow customers to monitor their laundry cycles remotely.

Here are some examples of smart laundry solutions:

- **Smart Washers and Dryers:** These machines are equipped with sensors and connectivity features that allow users to control and monitor them remotely through a mobile app. Customers can start, stop, or pause cycles, receive notifications when their laundry is done, and even troubleshoot issues remotely.
- **Mobile Apps:** Laundromat mobile apps allow customers to find nearby laundromats, check

machine availability, pay for services, and track their laundry progress. Some apps even offer loyalty programs, discounts, and personalized recommendations.
- **Smart Detergent Dispensers:** These dispensers automatically dispense the correct amount of detergent and fabric softener based on the load size and cycle selected. This eliminates the need for customers to measure detergent and reduces waste.
- **Smart Laundry Baskets:** These baskets are equipped with sensors that can weigh laundry and recommend the appropriate machine size and cycle. Some smart baskets can even connect to mobile apps to track laundry progress and send notifications when the cycle is complete.

Smart Dry Cleaning: This involves using technology to streamline the dry cleaning process, from garment tagging and tracking to automated stain removal and quality control. This can improve efficiency, reduce errors, and enhance the overall quality of service.

- **Self-Service Kiosks:** These kiosks allow customers to check in their laundry for wash-and-fold services, pay for services, and track their order status. This reduces wait times and frees up staff to focus on other tasks.
- **Cashless Payment Systems:** Implement cashless payment systems that allow customers to pay for services using their smartphones, credit cards, or digital wallets. This eliminates

the need for cash handling and reduces the risk of theft or fraud.
- **Energy Monitoring Systems:** Use energy monitoring systems to track energy usage and identify opportunities for conservation. This can help you reduce your operating costs and improve your environmental footprint.
- **Remote Troubleshooting:** Some smart laundry solutions allow for remote troubleshooting of machine issues, minimizing downtime and reducing the need for on-site repairs.

By embracing smart laundry solutions, you can enhance the customer experience, improve efficiency, and reduce costs. These technologies can differentiate your laundromat from the competition, attract tech-savvy customers, and position your business for long-term success.

10.5 Enhancing Customer Experience with Technology

Technology can play a pivotal role in enhancing the customer experience at your laundromat. By incorporating innovative solutions, you can create a more convenient, engaging, and enjoyable laundry day for your customers.

Here are some ways to enhance the customer experience with technology:

- **Free Wi-Fi:** Offer complimentary Wi-Fi to allow customers to browse the internet, check emails,

or stream videos while they wait for their laundry. This can make the wait more enjoyable and encourage customers to spend more time in your laundromat, potentially increasing revenue from vending machines or other services.
- **Charging Stations:** Provide charging stations for phones, laptops, or other electronic devices. This thoughtful amenity can be a lifesaver for customers who need to charge their devices while they wait.
- **Entertainment Options:** Install televisions or offer reading materials like magazines or newspapers to keep customers entertained during their laundry session. You could also create a playlist of upbeat music to create a lively atmosphere.
- **Interactive Displays:** Consider installing interactive displays that provide customers with information about your services, promotions, or local events. This can be a fun and engaging way to interact with customers and promote your brand.
- **Mobile App:** Develop a mobile app for your laundromat that allows customers to check machine availability, pay for services, track their laundry progress, and receive notifications when their cycle is complete. This can enhance convenience and streamline the laundry experience.
- **Loyalty Programs:** Use technology to implement a loyalty program that rewards customers for their repeat business. This could

involve offering discounts, free washes, or exclusive perks based on points earned through purchases or referrals.
- **Feedback and Reviews:** Use technology to gather feedback from customers through online surveys, feedback forms, or social media. This can help you identify areas for improvement and tailor your services to meet customer needs.
- **Smart Lockers:** Install smart lockers that allow customers to securely store their belongings while they wait for their laundry. This can provide peace of mind and enhance the overall security of your laundromat.

By integrating technology into the customer experience, you can create a modern, convenient, and enjoyable environment that differentiates your laundromat from the competition and fosters customer loyalty.

10.6 Staying Ahead of the Curve with Innovation

The laundromat industry is constantly evolving, with new technologies and innovations emerging at a rapid pace. Staying ahead of the curve is essential for maintaining a competitive edge and providing your customers with the latest and greatest laundry solutions.

Here are some tips for staying ahead of the curve with innovation:

- **Attend Industry Events:** Attend industry trade shows, conferences, and workshops to learn about new products, technologies, and trends. Network with other laundromat owners and suppliers to gather insights and stay informed about the latest developments.
- **Read Industry Publications:** Subscribe to industry publications like American Coin-Op, Planet Laundry, or Coin Laundry Association newsletters to stay abreast of the latest news, trends, and best practices in the laundromat industry.
- **Join Online Communities:** Participate in online forums and communities for laundromat owners to share ideas, ask questions, and learn from the experiences of others. This can be a valuable resource for discovering new technologies and innovative solutions.
- **Follow Industry Leaders:** Follow industry leaders, suppliers, and other innovative laundromats on social media to stay informed about their latest offerings and best practices.
- **Experiment with New Technologies:** Don't be afraid to experiment with new technologies to see how they can improve your operations and enhance the customer experience. This could involve testing new mobile payment options, trying out smart laundry solutions, or implementing a new customer loyalty program.
- **Seek Feedback from Customers:** Regularly solicit feedback from your customers to understand their needs, preferences, and pain

points. This can help you identify areas where you can innovate and improve your services.
- **Invest in Research and Development:** Allocate a portion of your budget to research and development to explore new technologies and innovations that could benefit your laundromat. This could involve partnering with technology companies, conducting customer surveys, or experimenting with pilot programs.

By embracing innovation and staying ahead of the curve, you can position your laundromat as a leader in the industry, attract tech-savvy customers, and ensure long-term growth and success.

10.7 Embracing Eco-Friendly Practices

As environmental concerns continue to grow, embracing eco-friendly practices is becoming increasingly important for businesses in all industries, including laundromats. By adopting sustainable practices, you can reduce your environmental impact, appeal to eco-conscious customers, and potentially save money on operating costs.

Here are some eco-friendly practices you can implement in your laundromat:

- **Energy-Efficient Equipment:** Invest in ENERGY STAR certified washers and dryers that use less water and electricity. Consider using high-spin washers to reduce drying times and energy consumption.

- **Water Recycling:** Install a water recycling system that filters and reuses wastewater for certain laundry cycles. This can significantly reduce your water consumption and lower your utility bills.
- **Heat Recovery Systems:** Implement heat recovery systems that capture waste heat from dryers and use it to preheat incoming water for washers. This can significantly reduce energy consumption and lower heating costs.
- **LED Lighting:** Replace traditional light bulbs with energy-efficient LED lighting. LEDs use less energy and last longer, resulting in long-term savings and reduced environmental impact.
- **Renewable Energy:** If feasible, consider installing solar panels or other renewable energy sources to power your laundromat. This can significantly reduce your reliance on fossil fuels and lower your carbon footprint.
- **Eco-Friendly Laundry Products:** Use and sell eco-friendly laundry products, such as biodegradable detergents and fabric softeners. Offer incentives for customers who bring their own reusable laundry bags.
- **Water Conservation:** Encourage customers to use full loads and choose shorter wash cycles to conserve water. Repair any leaks or drips promptly to prevent water waste.
- **Recycling:** Provide recycling bins for plastic bottles, aluminum cans, and cardboard boxes. This can help reduce waste and promote a more sustainable environment.

- **Education:** Educate your customers about the importance of eco-friendly laundry practices through signage, brochures, or workshops. Highlight your laundromat's commitment to sustainability and encourage customers to do their part.

By embracing eco-friendly practices, you can not only reduce your environmental impact but also attract a growing segment of eco-conscious consumers who prioritize sustainability. This can enhance your brand image, build customer loyalty, and contribute to a healthier planet.

Chapter 11

Overcoming Challenges and Troubleshooting – Weathering the Storms of Laundromat Ownership

Welcome back, laundry warriors! You've navigated the initial phases of launching and operating your laundromat, and now it's time to face the inevitable: challenges. Every business encounters obstacles, and laundromats are no exception. But fear not, for this chapter is your survival guide, equipping you with the knowledge and strategies to overcome challenges, troubleshoot issues, and emerge stronger than ever.

In the world of laundry, challenges can range from equipment malfunctions and disgruntled customers to fierce competition and unexpected economic downturns. This chapter will delve into these common hurdles, providing you with practical solutions, troubleshooting tips, and a healthy dose of resilience to weather any storm that comes your way.

So, buckle up and prepare to face the challenges head-on, armed with the knowledge and confidence to overcome them and keep your laundromat running smoothly.

11.1 Dealing with Equipment Malfunctions

Equipment malfunctions are an inevitable part of running a laundromat. Washers break down, dryers overheat, and change machines jam. While these occurrences can be frustrating, it's crucial to have a plan in place to address them promptly and efficiently.

Here's how to handle equipment malfunctions:

1. **Regular Maintenance:** The best way to prevent equipment malfunctions is to schedule regular maintenance for all your machines. This includes cleaning lint traps, inspecting hoses and belts, lubricating moving parts, and checking for signs of wear and tear. Refer to the manufacturer's instructions for recommended maintenance schedules.
2. **Troubleshooting Guide:** Create a troubleshooting guide for common machine issues, such as leaks, strange noises, or error codes. This guide can help your staff or a technician quickly diagnose and resolve problems.
3. **Service Contracts:** Consider purchasing service contracts for your equipment. These contracts often include preventive maintenance and priority service for repairs, minimizing downtime and ensuring prompt resolution of issues.
4. **Spare Parts Inventory:** Keep a stock of essential spare parts on hand, such as belts, hoses, and fuses, to enable quick repairs. This can save you

time and money by avoiding delays in ordering parts.
5. **Emergency Contact List:** Create a list of emergency contact numbers for your equipment suppliers, technicians, and other service providers. This will allow you to quickly reach out for help in case of a breakdown.
6. **Communication with Customers:** If a machine breaks down while a customer is using it, be transparent and apologetic. Offer a refund or a free wash to compensate for the inconvenience. Communicate clearly about the expected repair time and offer alternative solutions if possible.
7. **Regular Inspections:** Conduct regular inspections of all equipment to identify any potential issues before they escalate into major malfunctions. Look for signs of wear and tear, leaks, or unusual noises.
8. **Proper Training:** Train your staff on how to operate and maintain the equipment properly. This can help prevent user errors that could lead to malfunctions.

By being proactive and prepared, you can minimize the impact of equipment malfunctions on your business and ensure a positive experience for your customers.

11.2 Handling Difficult Customers

Dealing with difficult customers is an unavoidable part of running any business, and laundromats are no exception. Whether it's a customer who is upset about a broken machine, a lost item, or a perceived injustice, it's important to handle these situations calmly, professionally, and effectively.

Here are some tips for handling difficult customers:

1. **Listen Actively:** Let the customer vent their frustrations without interrupting or becoming defensive. Listen attentively to their concerns and acknowledge their feelings.
2. **Empathize:** Show empathy for the customer's situation and let them know you understand their frustration. Avoid making excuses or blaming others.
3. **Apologize:** Offer a sincere apology for the inconvenience caused, even if the issue wasn't directly your fault. A genuine apology can often de-escalate a tense situation.
4. **Offer Solutions:** Work with the customer to find a solution that addresses their concerns. This could involve offering a refund, a discount, or a free wash. Be flexible and willing to compromise to find a resolution that satisfies both parties.
5. **Stay Calm and Professional:** Maintain your composure even if the customer becomes angry or aggressive. Avoid raising your voice or getting into an argument. If the situation escalates, politely ask the customer to leave or call security if necessary.
6. **Document the Incident:** After the interaction, document the details of the incident, including the customer's name, contact information, the

nature of the complaint, and the resolution. This can be helpful for future reference and training purposes.
7. **Learn from the Experience:** Use difficult customer interactions as an opportunity to learn and improve your customer service. Identify any areas where your policies or procedures may need to be adjusted to prevent similar issues from arising in the future.
8. **Train Your Staff:** Train your staff on how to handle difficult customers effectively. Role-playing scenarios can be helpful for practicing de-escalation techniques and problem-solving skills.

By handling difficult customers with empathy, professionalism, and a willingness to find solutions, you can turn a negative experience into a positive one, potentially earning their loyalty and respect.

11.3 Managing Competition

Competition is a natural part of the business world, and the laundromat industry is no exception. Whether you're facing established laundromats or new entrants in the market, it's essential to have a strategy for managing competition and staying ahead of the game.

Here are some tips for managing competition:

1. **Know Your Competitors:** Research your competitors thoroughly. Visit their laundromats, analyze their pricing, services, and amenities, and identify their strengths and

weaknesses. This information will help you differentiate your laundromat and create a unique value proposition.

2. **Differentiate Your Laundromat:** Find ways to stand out from the competition. This could involve offering unique services like wash-and-fold, dry cleaning, or pet-friendly washing. You could also focus on creating a more inviting and comfortable atmosphere, offering extended hours, or providing exceptional customer service.

3. **Build a Strong Brand:** Develop a strong brand identity that resonates with your target audience and differentiates you from the competition. This includes your logo, color scheme, messaging, and overall aesthetic. Create a consistent brand experience across all touchpoints, from your website and social media profiles to your in-store signage and customer interactions.

4. **Offer Competitive Pricing:** While undercutting your competitors on price may not be sustainable in the long run, it's important to offer competitive pricing that reflects the value of your services. Consider offering special promotions, discounts, or loyalty programs to attract and retain customers.

5. **Focus on Customer Service:** Exceptional customer service can set you apart from the competition and build a loyal customer base. Train your staff to be friendly, helpful, and responsive to customer needs. Address any

complaints or issues promptly and professionally.
6. **Stay Up-to-Date on Industry Trends:** Keep up with the latest trends and innovations in the laundromat industry. This could involve attending industry trade shows, reading industry publications, or joining online communities for laundromat owners. By staying informed, you can adapt your business to meet changing customer needs and stay ahead of the competition.
7. **Market Your Laundromat Effectively:** Develop a comprehensive marketing strategy to promote your laundromat and attract new customers. Utilize online and offline advertising, social media, community events, and partnerships with local businesses to increase your visibility and reach your target audience.

By implementing these strategies, you can effectively manage competition and position your laundromat for long-term success.

11.4 Adapting to Economic Fluctuations

The economy is constantly changing, and laundromat owners must be prepared to adapt to economic fluctuations to ensure the sustainability of their business. Economic downturns can impact consumer spending habits, leading to decreased demand for laundry services. However, laundromats are generally considered recession-resistant businesses, as people still need to wash their clothes even during tough times.

Here are some strategies for adapting to economic fluctuations:

1. **Cost Control:** During economic downturns, it's crucial to control costs and manage expenses effectively. This could involve negotiating better rates with suppliers, reducing energy consumption, optimizing staffing levels, or cutting back on discretionary spending.
2. **Diversify Revenue Streams:** Explore additional revenue streams to offset any potential decline in self-service laundry usage. This could involve offering wash-and-fold services, dry cleaning, or other value-added services that cater to a broader range of customer needs.
3. **Promotional Offers:** During slow periods, consider offering special promotions or discounts to incentivize customers to visit your laundromat. This could include discounted wash cycles, bundled services, or loyalty rewards.
4. **Focus on Customer Retention:** Invest in building strong relationships with your existing customers. Offer excellent customer service, personalized attention, and loyalty programs to encourage repeat business.
5. **Adapt to Changing Needs:** Be flexible and adaptable to changing customer needs and preferences. For example, if customers are looking for more affordable options during an

economic downturn, you could offer budget-friendly wash cycles or bulk discounts.

Stay Informed: Keep abreast of economic trends and forecasts to anticipate any potential impact on your business. This will allow you to proactively adjust your strategies and prepare for any potential challenges.

7. **Seek Government Assistance:** In times of economic hardship, the government may offer assistance programs for small businesses, such as loans, grants, or tax breaks. Research these programs and see if you qualify for any assistance.

By being proactive, adaptable, and customer-focused, you can navigate economic fluctuations and ensure the long-term viability of your laundromat.

11.5 Addressing Security Concerns

Security is a critical aspect of running a laundromat. Unfortunately, laundromats can be targets for theft, vandalism, and other security incidents. Implementing robust security measures is essential for protecting your investment, ensuring the safety of your customers and staff, and maintaining a positive reputation.

Here are some tips for addressing security concerns in your laundromat:

- **Security Cameras:** Install high-resolution security cameras in strategic locations throughout your laundromat, both inside and outside. Ensure cameras are visible and cover all areas, including entrances, exits, laundry areas, folding tables, and parking lots. Consider using cameras with night vision and remote viewing capabilities for 24/7 surveillance.

- **Alarm Systems:** Install a reliable alarm system that includes door and window sensors, motion detectors, and a loud siren. Connect the alarm system to a central monitoring station for immediate response in case of a security breach.
- **Secure Entry and Exit Points:** Use sturdy locks on doors and windows to prevent unauthorized access. Consider installing a buzzer system for after-hours entry, allowing you to screen visitors before granting access.
- **Lighting:** Ensure adequate lighting both inside and outside your laundromat. Well-lit areas deter criminal activity and create a sense of safety for customers and staff.
- **Security Personnel:** If your budget allows, consider hiring security personnel to patrol your laundromat, especially during late-night hours or in high-crime areas.
- **Employee Training:** Train your staff on security protocols, including how to respond to suspicious activity, handle emergencies, and de-escalate conflicts. Ensure they know how to operate the security cameras and alarm system.
- **Cash Handling Procedures:** Implement secure cash handling procedures to minimize the risk of theft. Limit the amount of cash on hand, use a drop safe, and deposit cash regularly at the bank.

- **Signage:** Post clear signage reminding customers to be vigilant about their belongings and report any suspicious activity to staff.
- **Regular Inspections:** Conduct regular inspections of your premises to identify and address any potential security vulnerabilities. Check for broken locks, faulty lighting, or any other issues that could compromise security.
- **Community Engagement:** Build relationships with local law enforcement and community organizations to enhance security and deter crime. Participate in neighborhood watch programs or business improvement districts.

By implementing a multi-layered approach to security, you can create a safe and secure environment for your customers and staff, protect your investment, and minimize the risk of theft, vandalism, or other security incidents.

11.6 Maintaining High Hygiene Standards

Laundromats are inherently susceptible to germs and bacteria due to the constant handling of dirty laundry and the use of shared equipment. Maintaining high hygiene standards is crucial for ensuring the health and safety of your customers and staff, as well as protecting your reputation as a clean and trustworthy establishment.

Here are some essential hygiene practices for laundromats:

- **Machine Cleaning and Disinfection:** Regularly clean and disinfect the interiors and exteriors of all washing machines and dryers. Use a disinfectant cleaner that is effective against a broad spectrum of bacteria and viruses. Pay special attention to high-touch areas like door handles, control panels, and detergent dispensers.
- **Surface Cleaning:** Clean and disinfect all surfaces, including folding tables, countertops, chairs, and floors, using a disinfectant cleaner. Wipe down surfaces after each use and clean them more thoroughly at the end of each day.
- **Restroom Sanitation:** Clean and disinfect restrooms multiple times a day, paying special attention to toilets, sinks, faucets, and door handles. Restock toilet paper, paper towels, soap, and hand sanitizer regularly.
- **Air Quality:** Ensure proper ventilation to maintain good air quality and prevent the buildup of moisture, which can promote the growth of mold and mildew. Regularly clean air vents and replace air filters.
- **Laundry Cart Sanitation:** Sanitize laundry carts and baskets after each use to prevent the spread of germs.
- **Hand Hygiene:** Encourage customers and staff to wash their hands frequently with soap and water or use hand sanitizer. Provide hand sanitizing stations throughout the laundromat.
- **Employee Training:** Train your staff on proper cleaning and disinfection procedures. Ensure

they understand the importance of hygiene and follow protocols consistently.
- **Signage:** Post clear signage reminding customers and staff to wash their hands, cover their coughs and sneezes, and practice good hygiene.

By adhering to strict hygiene standards, you can create a clean and healthy environment for your customers and staff, minimize the risk of illness, and maintain a positive reputation for your laundromat.

11.7 Resolving Operational Issues

Even with meticulous planning and preparation, operational issues can arise in any business, and laundromats are no exception. These issues can range from minor inconveniences like a jammed change machine to more significant problems like a power outage or a major equipment malfunction.

Here's how to effectively resolve operational issues:

- **Have a Plan:** Develop a contingency plan for common operational issues. This could include having a backup generator for power outages, a list of emergency repair services, or a plan for communicating with customers during unexpected closures.
- **Be Proactive:** Don't wait for problems to arise. Regularly inspect your equipment, monitor your supplies, and address any potential issues before they escalate.

- **Act Quickly:** When an issue does arise, act quickly to resolve it. This may involve calling a repair technician, contacting your supplier, or implementing a temporary workaround.
- **Communicate with Customers:** Keep customers informed about any operational issues that may affect their experience. Post signs, send emails, or update your social media channels to communicate the issue and estimated resolution time.
- **Offer Solutions:** If the issue inconveniences customers, offer solutions such as refunds, discounts, or free washes. This shows that you value their business and are committed to resolving the issue promptly.
- **Learn from Mistakes:** Use operational issues as an opportunity to learn and improve your processes. Analyze what went wrong and implement changes to prevent similar issues from happening again.
- **Seek Help:** Don't hesitate to seek help from professionals if you need assistance resolving a complex issue. This could involve calling a technician, consulting with an attorney, or reaching out to your insurance provider.

By addressing operational issues proactively, communicating transparently with customers, and seeking help when needed, you can minimize the impact of these issues on your business and maintain a positive customer experience.

Chapter 12

Scaling and Expanding Your Laundromat Empire – From Single Spin Cycle to Laundry Dynasty

Congratulations, laundry magnates! You've successfully launched your laundromat, mastered the day-to-day operations, overcome challenges, and built a loyal customer base. Now it's time to set your sights on the horizon and embark on an exciting new phase: scaling and expanding your laundromat empire.

This is where your entrepreneurial dreams take flight, where your single laundromat evolves into a thriving network of laundry havens. In this chapter, we'll explore the various pathways to growth, from opening additional locations and franchising your brand to exploring new revenue streams and investing in cutting-edge technology. We'll also discuss the importance of building a strong team, cultivating leadership skills, and leaving a lasting legacy in the laundry industry.

So, fasten your seatbelts and prepare for an exhilarating journey as we delve into the strategies and tactics that will propel your laundromat from a single spin cycle to a full-fledged laundry dynasty.

12.1 Evaluating Growth Opportunities

Before you embark on any expansion plans, it's crucial to evaluate your current business and identify potential growth opportunities. This involves analyzing your financial performance, assessing market demand, and considering your resources and capabilities.

Here's a step-by-step guide to evaluating growth opportunities for your laundromat:

1. **Financial Analysis:** Review your financial statements, including your income statement, balance sheet, and cash flow statement, to assess your current financial health and profitability. Analyze key metrics like revenue growth, profit margins, and return on investment (ROI) to determine your financial capacity for expansion.
2. **Market Research:** Conduct thorough market research to identify potential areas for growth. Look for underserved areas with a high demand for laundry services, such as densely populated neighborhoods, college towns, or areas with a large immigrant population. Assess the competitive landscape and identify any gaps in the market that you can fill.
3. **Customer Feedback:** Gather feedback from your customers to understand their needs, preferences, and suggestions for improvement. This can provide valuable insights into potential

new services or amenities you could offer to attract a wider audience.
4. **SWOT Analysis:** Conduct a SWOT analysis (Strengths, Weaknesses, Opportunities, Threats) to assess your laundromat's internal strengths and weaknesses, as well as external opportunities and threats. This will help you identify areas where you can leverage your strengths to capitalize on opportunities and mitigate risks.
5. **Resource Assessment:** Evaluate your available resources, including financial capital, staff, equipment, and expertise. Determine if you have the necessary resources to support your growth plans or if you need to secure additional funding or partnerships.
6. **Scalability:** Assess the scalability of your business model. Can your current operations be easily replicated in new locations? Do you have systems and processes in place to manage multiple laundromats efficiently?

By carefully evaluating these factors, you can identify the most promising growth opportunities for your laundromat and develop a strategic plan for expansion.

12.2 Opening Additional Locations

One of the most common ways to expand a laundromat business is to open additional locations. This allows you to reach a wider audience, increase your market share, and generate more revenue.

However, opening new locations requires careful planning, significant investment, and a well-thought-out strategy.

Here are some key considerations for opening additional laundromat locations:

- **Location Selection:** The location of your new laundromat is crucial for its success. Choose a location that is easily accessible, has high visibility, and is located in an area with a strong demand for laundry services. Consider factors like demographics, competition, and foot traffic when evaluating potential locations.
- **Market Research:** Conduct thorough market research to understand the specific needs and preferences of your target audience in the new location. This will help you tailor your services, pricing, and marketing efforts accordingly.
- **Financial Projections:** Develop detailed financial projections for your new location, including startup costs, operating expenses, and revenue forecasts. This will help you determine the financial viability of the project and secure funding if needed.
- **Operational Efficiency:** Implement standardized systems and processes across all your locations to ensure consistency, efficiency, and quality control. This could include using the same laundromat management software, training programs, and cleaning protocols.
- **Marketing and Branding:** Create a cohesive brand identity across all your locations to build

brand recognition and loyalty. Develop targeted marketing campaigns to promote your new location and attract customers.
- **Staffing:** Hire and train qualified staff to manage your new location. Consider promoting existing employees to managerial positions to ensure a smooth transition and maintain your company culture.
- **Logistics:** Manage the logistics of opening a new location, including lease negotiations, equipment procurement, permits and licenses, and construction or renovation.

By carefully planning and executing your expansion strategy, you can successfully open additional laundromat locations, expand your reach, and increase your market share.

12.3 Franchising Your Laundromat Business

Franchising is another popular way to expand a successful laundromat business. It allows you to leverage your brand, systems, and expertise to rapidly grow your business without the need for significant capital investment. In a franchise model, you grant independent entrepreneurs the right to operate a laundromat under your brand name and business model in exchange for an initial fee and ongoing royalties.

Here's how franchising works:

1. **Develop a Franchise Model:** Create a comprehensive franchise model that outlines

your brand standards, operating procedures, marketing strategies, and financial requirements for franchisees.
2. **Recruit Franchisees:** Market your franchise opportunity to potential investors who are looking to own and operate their own laundromat. Conduct thorough interviews to select qualified franchisees who are committed to upholding your brand standards and values.
3. **Provide Training and Support:** Offer comprehensive training and ongoing support to your franchisees to ensure they have the knowledge and resources to successfully operate their laundromats. This could include training on equipment operation and maintenance, customer service, marketing, and financial management.
4. **Monitor Performance:** Regularly monitor the performance of your franchisees to ensure they are adhering to your brand standards and meeting performance goals. Provide feedback and support to help them improve their operations.
5. **Collect Royalties:** Collect royalties from your franchisees, which are typically a percentage of their gross sales. This provides you with a steady stream of income and allows you to continue investing in the growth and development of your brand.

Franchising can be a powerful growth strategy for laundromat businesses that have a proven track record, a strong brand identity, and a well-defined business model. It allows you to expand rapidly, reach new markets, and generate recurring revenue without having to invest your own capital in new locations.

12.4 Exploring New Revenue Streams

Expanding your laundromat business doesn't always mean opening new locations or franchising. You can also explore new revenue streams to diversify your income and increase profitability.

Here are some potential new revenue streams for your laundromat:

- **Wash-and-Fold Services:** Offer wash-and-fold services where customers drop off their laundry to be washed, dried, and folded by your staff. This convenient service is popular among busy professionals, families, and students.
- **Dry Cleaning:** Partner with a local dry cleaner or invest in your own dry-cleaning equipment to offer this premium service. Dry cleaning caters to customers with delicate or specialty garments that require special care.
- **Ironing and Pressing:** Offer ironing and pressing services for customers who want their clothes to look crisp and professional.
- **Alterations and Repairs:** Partner with a seamstress or tailor to offer alteration and repair services for clothing and other textiles.
- **Shoe Repair and Cleaning:** Partner with a shoe repair specialist to offer shoe cleaning, polishing, and repair services.

- **Vending Machines:** Expand your vending machine offerings beyond snacks and drinks. Consider adding laundry supplies like detergent, fabric softener, and dryer sheets. You could also offer other essentials like phone chargers, headphones, or travel-sized toiletries.
- **Pickup and Delivery:** Offer pickup and delivery services for added convenience, especially for customers who are elderly, disabled, or simply too busy to visit your laundromat.
- **Commercial Laundry:** Cater to local businesses by offering commercial laundry services for items like uniforms, linens, and towels.
- **Laundromat Café:** Create a café within your laundromat where customers can enjoy coffee, snacks, or light meals while they wait for their laundry. This can create a more inviting atmosphere and generate additional revenue.
- **Events and Workshops:** Host laundry-related events or workshops, such as stain removal workshops, laundry care classes, or "laundry and learn" sessions. This can attract new customers, build community, and generate revenue from ticket sales or sponsorships.

By exploring new revenue streams, you can diversify your income, cater to a broader range of customer needs, and increase the overall profitability of your laundromat.

www.ingramcontent.com/pod-product-compliance
Lightning Source LLC
Chambersburg PA
CBHW071923210526
45479CB00002B/531